BRITISH BATTLES

getmapping® + HarperCollins*Publishers*

BRITISH BATTLES

First published in 2002 by
HarperCollinsPublishers
77–85 Fulham Palace Road
London W6 8JB

The HarperCollins website address is:
www.fireandwater.com

Photography © 2002 Getmapping plc

Getmapping can produce an individual print of any area shown in this
book, or of any area within the United Kingdom. The image can be
centred wherever you choose, printed at any size from A6 to 7.5 metres
square, and at any scale up to 1:1,000. For further information, please
contact Getmapping on 0845 0551550, or log on to www.getmapping.com

The publisher regrets that it can accept no responsibility for any errors
or omissions within this publication, or for any expense of loss thereby
caused.

A CIP catalogue record for this book is available from the British Library.

ISBN: 0 00 714417 2

Text by Ian Harrison
Design and Cartography by Martin Brown
Original Cartography by Peter Harper
Photographic image processing by Getmapping plc
Colour origination by Colourscan, Singapore
Printed and bound in Great Britain by Butler and Tanner Ltd

contents

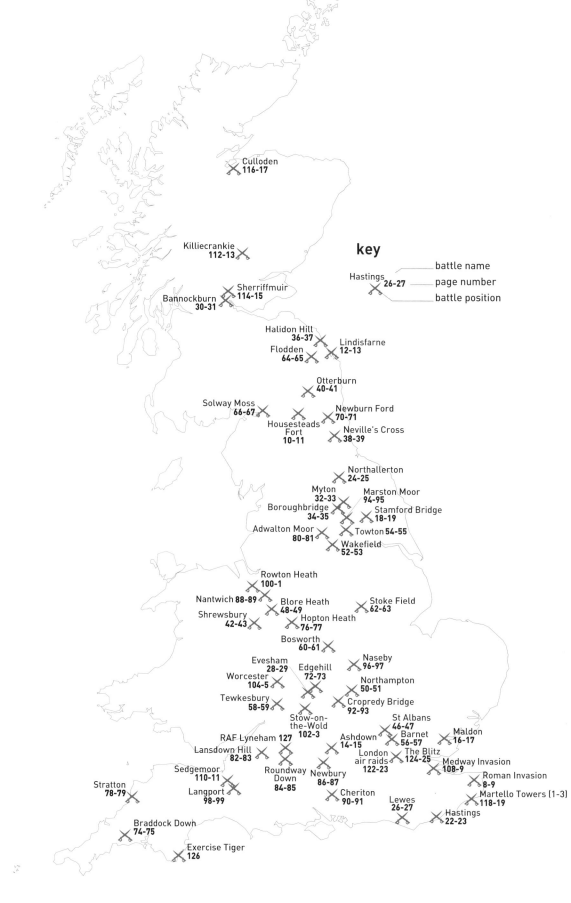

Culloden
116-17

Killiecrankie
112-13

key

Hastings .... battle name
26-27 .... page number
battle position

Sherriffmuir
114-15

Bannockburn
30-31

Halidon Hill
36-37
Lindisfarne
12-13
Flodden
64-65

Otterburn
40-41

Solway Moss
66-67
Newburn Ford
70-71
Housesteads
Fort
10-11
Neville's Cross
38-39

Northallerton
24-25

Myton
32-33
Marston Moor
94-95
Boroughbridge
34-35
Stamford Bridge
18-19
Adwalton Moor
80-81
Towton **54-55**
Wakefield
52-53

Rowton Heath
100-1

Nantwich **88-89**
Blore Heath
48-49
Stoke Field
62-63
Shrewsbury
42-43
Hopton Heath
76-77

Bosworth
60-61

Evesham
28-29
Edgehill
72-73
Naseby
96-97
Worcester
104-5
Northampton
50-51
Tewkesbury
58-59
Cropredy Bridge
92-93
Stow-on-
the-Wold
102-3
St Albans
46-47
Maldon
16-17
Ashdown
14-15
Barnet
56-57
RAF Lyneham **127**
London
air raids
122-23
The Blitz
124-25
Lansdown Hill
82-83
Medway Invasion
108-9
Sedgemoor
110-11
Roundway
Down
Newbury
86-87
Roman Invasion
8-9
Stratton
78-79
Langport
98-99
Cheriton
90-91
Martello Towers (1-3)
118-19
Lewes
26-27
Braddock Down
74-75
Hastings
22-23

Exercise Tiger
126

PRE-NORMAN INVASION

ROMAN INVASION
August 55 BC and July 54 BC

1. War: Roman Invasion
2. Opposing forces: Romans/Various Belgic tribes
3. Opposing commanders: Julius Caesar/
   Cassivellaunus
4. Strength of opposing forces: 2 legions (55BC)/5
   legions & 2,000 cavalry (54BC)
5. Number of casualties: Not recorded
6. Outcome: Roman withdrawal (55BC)/Roman victory
   (54BC)
7. Consequences: Having negotiated peace after the
   second invasion Caesar withdrew to Gaul but never
   consolidated his success because he was needed
   elsewhere in the empire

England Photographic Atlas: Page 182, 204

Caesar's first foray into Britain came in late August 55BC, when he landed on the south-east coast with the VIIth and Xth Legions. He anchored off Dover to await his cavalry but found the cliffs lined with British warriors, making a landing impossible. Caesar then sailed north to attempt a landing on the beaches between Walmer and Deal but found that the British were again waiting at the beaches. However, prompted by the impetuous action of the Standard Bearer of the Xth, who leapt into the sea alone, the legionaries followed him into the water and drove the Britons back from the beach. Before Caesar could capitalize on this success, a violent storm damaged his fleet and he was forced to withdraw. Veni, vidi.

The following year Caesar returned with a much larger force. His fleet landed unchallenged at Sandwich and advanced to meet the British who had retired to a river crossing thought to be the River Stour near Canterbury. From there the Romans drove the British back to a wooden fort at Bigbury and managed to oust them from the fort but again the weather intervened and the Romans retired temporarily to repair their fleet. The British regrouped under the leadership of Cassivellaunus but defeat in a confrontation with three of the Roman legions broke the British alliance and Cassivellaunus withdrew to fight a guerrilla war from his base at Wheathampstead in Hertfordshire. However, rival tribes, fearful of his growing power, betrayed him to the Romans, who destroyed his fortress with a two-pronged attack and forced terms with the erstwhile British leader. Vici.

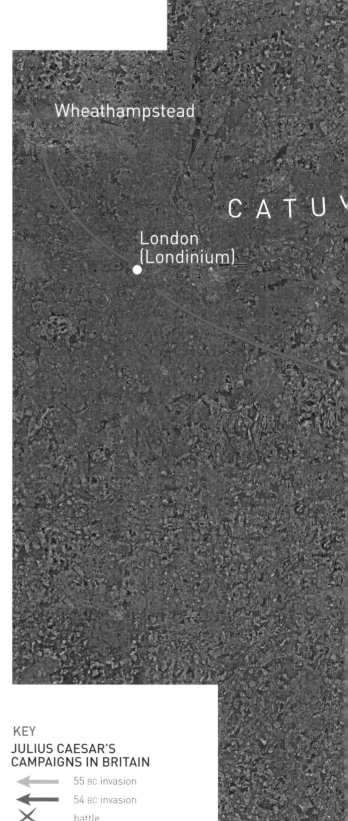

Wheathampstead

London
(Londinium)

C A T U V

ROMAN INVASION

Wheathampstead

LONDON

Canterbury

Royal Tunbridge
Wells

Dover

KEY
**JULIUS CAESAR'S
CAMPAIGNS IN BRITAIN**

55 BC invasion

54 BC invasion

battle

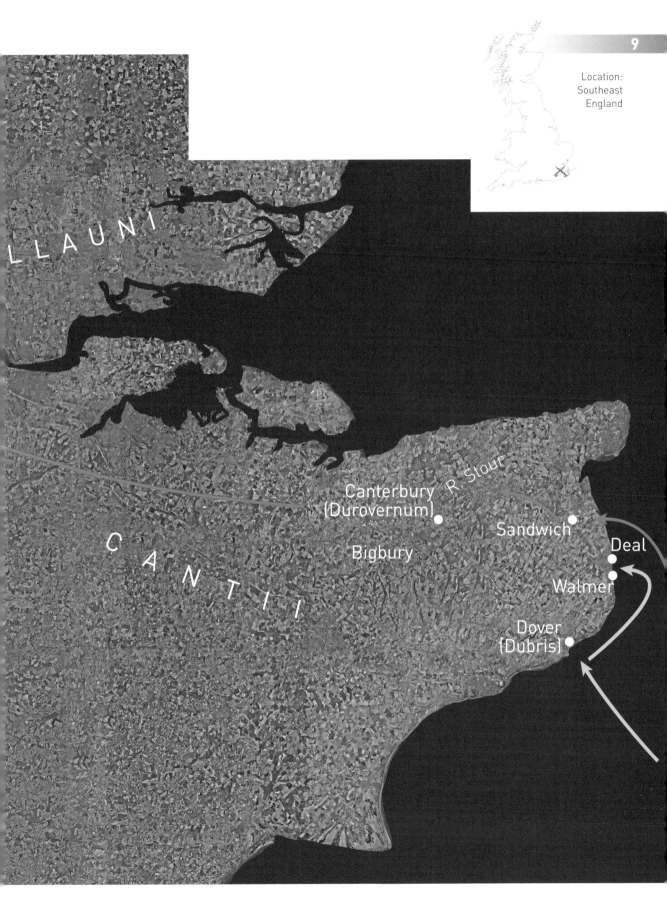

Location:
Southeast
England

LLAUNI

CANTII

Canterbury
(Durovernum)

R. Stour

Sandwich

Deal

Bigbury

Walmer

Dover
(Dubris)

HOUSESTEADS
C. AD 124

1. War: Roman Occupation
2. Opposing forces: Romans/Scots
3. Opposing commanders: Built at the behest of Emperor Hadrian/Various
4. Strength of opposing forces: Built by 3 legions
5. Number of casualties: n/a
6. Outcome: n/a
7. Consequences: The wall was built "to separate the barbarians from the Romans", and marked the northern limit of the Roman empire

England Photographic Atlas: Page 734, A5

Broomlee Lough

Distractions elsewhere in the Empire meant that the Romans did not capitalize on Caesar's success of 54BC (p. 8) until nearly a century later, in AD43, when the Emperor Claudius invaded Britain and began an occupation that was to last nearly 400 years. After half a century of expansion in Britain, Roman priorities turned to consolidation, which involved a withdrawal from the lowlands of Scotland to a line between the Solway and the Tyne. There was fierce fighting along this line from 118–122 and the Emperor Hadrian, on a visit to Britain in 122, ordered the building of what was to become Hadrian's Wall.

The wall was eighty miles long, running from Bowness on Solway in the west to Wallsend in the east, and was built in a mere seven years. It consisted of a stone barrier wall with wide ditches in front and behind, and was fortified with a fort or milecastle every mile along its length, with two watchtowers between each pair of milecastles. Seventeen garrison forts, accommodating between 500 and 1,000 men each, were also built so that the garrison could be stationed on the wall itself for immediate deployment. Housesteads, standing on the cliffs of Whin Sill, was one of these garrison forts and is Britain's most complete example of a Roman fort, now preserved by English Heritage.

Despite the enormous effort of building Hadrian's Wall, less than twenty years later Emperor Antoninus Pius decided to extend the empire northwards, building the 37-mile Antonine Wall from the Clyde to the Forth in 138. This wall was abandoned after Antoninus's death in 161, and from then until the Roman withdrawal in c. 409, Hadrian's Wall remained the northernmost limit of the empire.

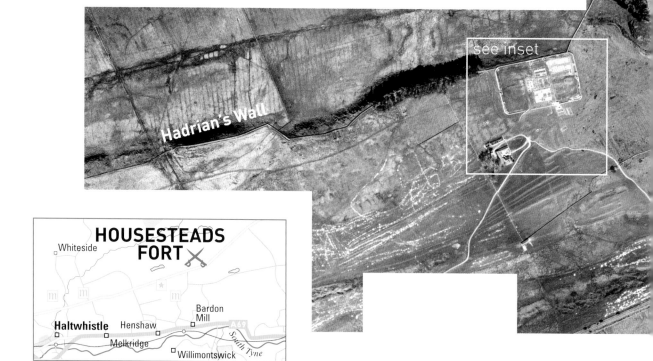

Hadrian's Wall

see inset

HOUSESTEADS FORT

Whiteside

Haltwhistle   Henshaw   Bardon Mill

Melkridge

Willimontswick

South Tyne

Hadrian's Wall

Hadrian's Wall

Location:
26 miles east
from the
centre of
Carlisle

Housesteads Fort

LINDISFARNE
8th June 793

1. War: Viking Incursions
2. Opposing forces: Northumbrians/Vikings
3. Opposing commanders: King Ethelred I of Northumbria/Not recorded
4. Strength of opposing forces: Not recorded
5. Number of casualties: Not recorded
6. Outcome: Viking victory
7. Consequences: Lindisfarne continued as a monastic centre for nearly a century after this attack but fear of the Vikings led the monks to flee the monastery in 875 for a safer location

England Photographic Atlas: Page 743, G2

The Viking attack on Lindisfarne was one of the earliest of a series of Viking raids that took place sporadically and with varying degrees of force between the 8th and the 11th centuries. The first recorded raid was in 789, the last serious incursion coming with the defeat of Harold Hardrada at Stamford Bridge in 1066 (p. 18).

On 8th June 793 Norwegian Vikings beached their longships on the North Shore of Lindisfarne (1) and sacked the monastery, killing many of the monks and taking others as slaves, as well as stripping the monastery of its rich treasures. This attack on an undefended monastery, "a place more venerable than all in Britain" was totally unexpected, and is recorded in the Anglo-Saxon Chronicle thus: "In this year dire portents appeared over Northumbria and sorely frightened the people. There were immense whirlwinds and flashes of lightening, and fiery dragons were seen flying in the air... and a little while after that the ravages of heathen men miserably destroyed God's church on Lindisfarne, with plunder and slaughter."

Location:
12 miles south
from Berwick-
upon-Tweed

P

castle

monastery

ASHDOWN
8th January 871

1. War: Viking Incursions
2. Opposing forces: Saxons/Vikings
3. Opposing commanders: King Aethelred of Wessex & his brother Alfred/Kings Bagsecg & Halfdan
4. Strength of opposing forces: Not recorded
5. Number of casualties: Not recorded
6. Outcome: Saxon victory
7. Consequences: Temporary relief in a war against the Danes that lasted until 878

England Photographic Atlas: Page 210, B2

From the middle of the 9th century, the pattern of Viking attacks began to change, with the Danes beginning to establish permanent settlements in England rather than simply making seasonal raids. Following this new pattern, the Viking Kings Bagsecg and Halfdan established a camp outside Reading in 870 and launched a concerted series of attacks against Wessex. King Aethelred of Wessex and his brother Alfred rallied their army to confront the Danes, and the two forces met on 8th January 871.

The Vikings marched out of their camp to meet the Saxons, and the two armies camped the night before the battle on the Ridgeway at Ashdown, close to the village of Aldworth on the Berkshire Downs. At dawn the Danes deployed their army in two divisions, one commanded by the two kings and the other by the Danish earls (1). Alfred and Aethelred's forces also formed two divisions (2) and, while Aethelred was offering prayers for victory, Alfred advanced to meet the Danish forces. A melee developed which was inconclusive until the late arrival of Aethelred, who had finished his prayers and now added to Alfred's might. Together they drove back the Danes, killing Bagsecg and securing victory.

Ashdown was a short-lived success, because the Saxons were defeated only two weeks later at Basing. The struggle continued until Alfred, who had by then succeeded his brother Aethelred as King, defeated the Danish King Guthrum at the Battle of Edington in 878 to secure peace on his terms and win the title Alfred the Great.

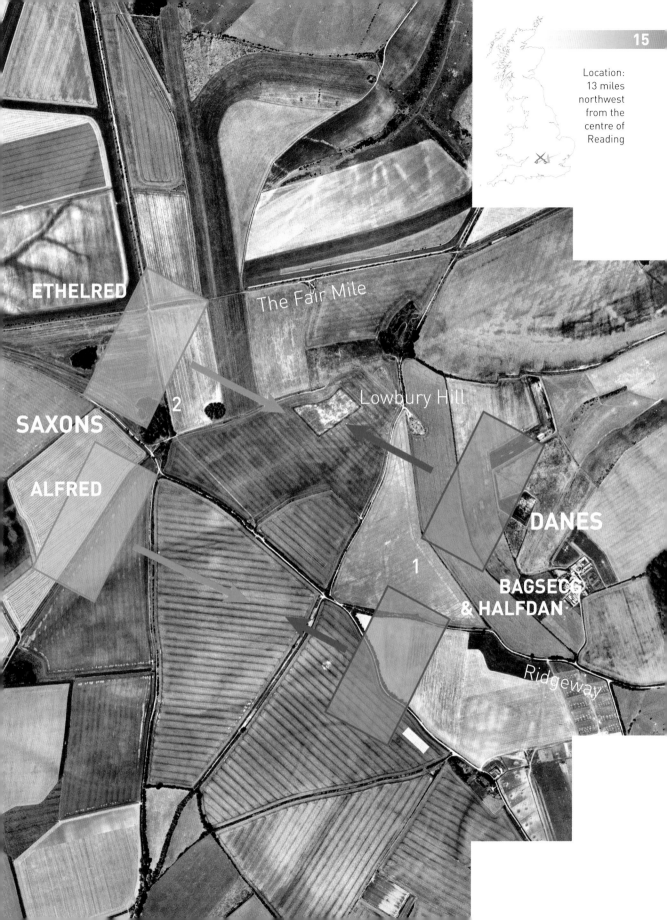

Location: 13 miles northwest from the centre of Reading

ETHELRED

The Fair Mile

SAXONS

Lowbury Hill

2

ALFRED

DANES

1

BAGSECG & HALFDAN

Ridgeway

MALDON
10th August 991

1. War: Viking Incursions
2. Opposing forces: Saxons/Vikings
3. Opposing commanders: Ealdorman Brihtnoth/King Olaf Tryggvasson of Norway and Guthmund & Jostein of Denmark
4. Strength of opposing forces: Not recorded
5. Number of casualties: Not recorded
6. Outcome: Viking victory
7. Consequences: Start of the gafol (payments of tribute)

England Photographic Atlas: Page 287, G4

In 991 a fleet of Viking ships sailed up the River Blackwater and landed at Northey Island which, being linked to the mainland by a tidal causeway, made an easily defensible base for Viking raids on the Saxon treasure chambers at Maldon. They were confronted there on 10th August 991 by a Saxon force commanded by Brihtnoth, Ealdorman of Essex.

The Vikings made ready to cross to the mainland and the opposing forces waited for the receding tide to reveal the causeway (1). Brihtnoth held the western end of the causeway with just three warriors, forcing the Vikings to ask to be allowed to cross to the mainland. Strangely, Brihtnoth agreed to this request, ordering his forces to fall back and form a shield wall or "war hedge" (2), which the Vikings attacked in a wedge-like formation called a "svinfylka" or "swine-array" (3). The reason for Brihtnoth's decision to allow the Vikings to cross may have been that he had to engage them in battle: had he simply held them, the Vikings would have sailed away to menace another part of the coast.

The Saxon line held, and the Vikings fell back to regroup. As they did so a Danish warrior issued a personal challenge to the Saxon leader. Brihtnoth killed the first challenger but was injured as he killed a second and, as he sank to his knees, the Vikings closed in on him and cut his head from his shoulders, at which the Saxon militia fled the field. The result of this victory was that the Vikings demanded the first of the tribute payments known as gafol (often confused with the Danegeld, an army tax which became a regular levy from 1012–1051).

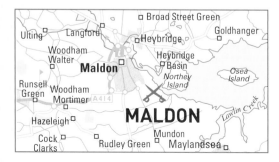

KEY

- Saxons
- Vikings
- viewpoint
- P car park

Location:
0.5 miles east
from the
centre of
Maldon

River Blackwater

Northey Island

causeway

Southey Creek

1

2

3

P

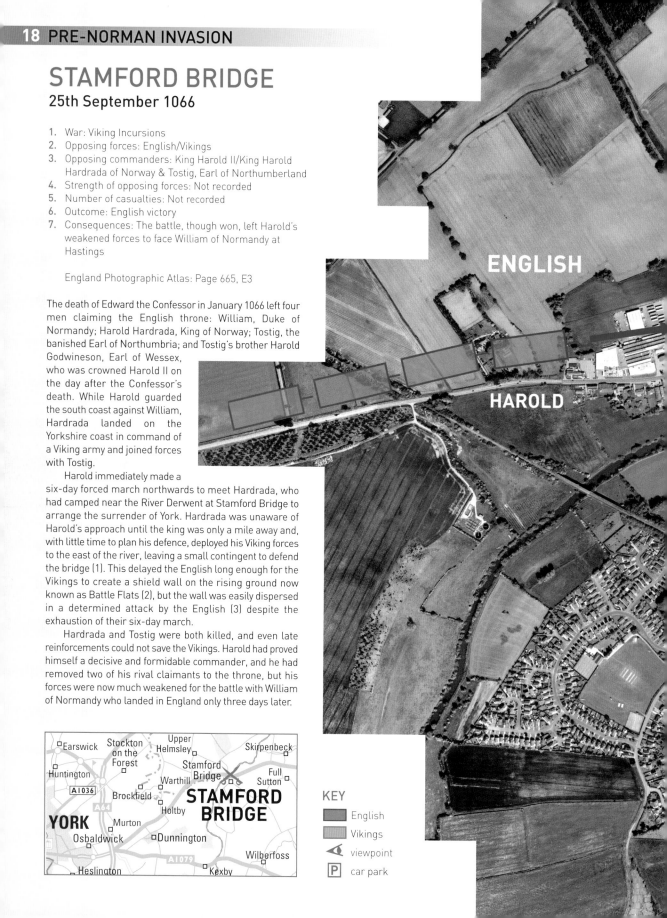

STAMFORD BRIDGE
25th September 1066

1. War: Viking Incursions
2. Opposing forces: English/Vikings
3. Opposing commanders: King Harold II/King Harold Hardrada of Norway & Tostig, Earl of Northumberland
4. Strength of opposing forces: Not recorded
5. Number of casualties: Not recorded
6. Outcome: English victory
7. Consequences: The battle, though won, left Harold's weakened forces to face William of Normandy at Hastings

England Photographic Atlas: Page 665, E3

The death of Edward the Confessor in January 1066 left four men claiming the English throne: William, Duke of Normandy; Harold Hardrada, King of Norway; Tostig, the banished Earl of Northumbria; and Tostig's brother Harold Godwineson, Earl of Wessex, who was crowned Harold II on the day after the Confessor's death. While Harold guarded the south coast against William, Hardrada landed on the Yorkshire coast in command of a Viking army and joined forces with Tostig.

Harold immediately made a six-day forced march northwards to meet Hardrada, who had camped near the River Derwent at Stamford Bridge to arrange the surrender of York. Hardrada was unaware of Harold's approach until the king was only a mile away and, with little time to plan his defence, deployed his Viking forces to the east of the river, leaving a small contingent to defend the bridge (1). This delayed the English long enough for the Vikings to create a shield wall on the rising ground now known as Battle Flats (2), but the wall was easily dispersed in a determined attack by the English (3) despite the exhaustion of their six-day march.

Hardrada and Tostig were both killed, and even late reinforcements could not save the Vikings. Harold had proved himself a decisive and formidable commander, and he had removed two of his rival claimants to the throne, but his forces were now much weakened for the battle with William of Normandy who landed in England only three days later.

ENGLISH

HAROLD

KEY

English
Vikings
◀ viewpoint
P car park

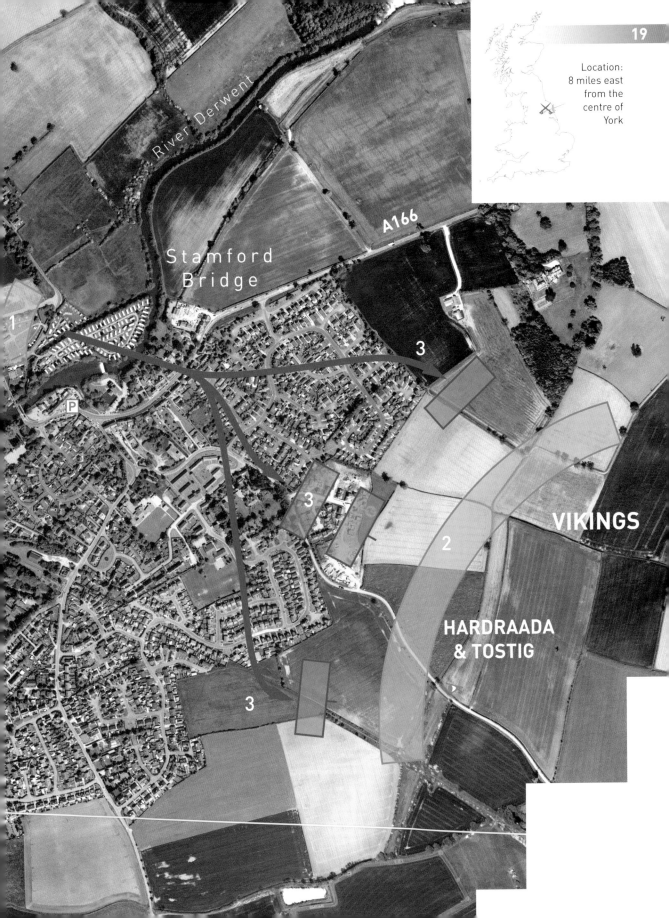

Location:
8 miles east
from the
centre of
York

River Derwent

A166

Stamford
Bridge

P

1

3

3

3

3

2

VIKINGS

HARDRAADA
& TOSTIG

HASTINGS TO THE WARS OF THE ROSES

HASTINGS
14th October 1066

1. War: Viking Incursions
2. Opposing forces: English/Normans
3. Opposing commanders: King Harold II/William, Duke of Normandy
4. Strength of opposing forces: 7,500 English 7,000 Normans
5. Number of casualties: 2,000 English/2,000 Normans
6. Outcome: Norman victory
7. Consequences: The "last English king" relinquished the throne and William was crowned Conqueror

England Photographic Atlas: Page 136, B2

Three days after Harold's victory at Stamford Bridge (p. 18), William, Duke of Normandy, landed at Pevensey with a force of 7,000 men. While William set up camp at Hastings, Harold marched south to London, marshalled fresh forces, and then marched into East Sussex. Perhaps hoping to surprise the Normans as he had the Vikings, Harold halted some distance from the Norman army, setting up camp at Senlac Ridge (now within the town of Battle). However, William heard news of Harold's arrival and, on the morning of 14th October, advanced to meet the English forces, reversing the advantage and surprising Harold.

But Harold had chosen a strong position on Senlac Ridge (1), protected from flanking attacks by the steep slopes of the ridge, and thereby forcing William to make a full frontal attack from his position across the valley on Telham Hill. Three times William's forces charged the English line and three times they recoiled. It is unclear whether the retreats were genuine or feigned but after the second withdrawal, parts of the English line made unauthorised and unsupported pursuits, only to be cut off in the valley and slaughtered by William's cavalry (2). As evening drew near, William, the aggressor in a foreign land, knew that he must secure victory to survive. He rallied his troops for a last attack, this time on Harold's personal standard. The standard bearer was killed, Harold's banner fell, and English morale collapsed with it. The line was broken, having held firm for eight hours, and four Norman knights came close enough to deliver mortal blows to the English king — the Duke of Normandy had earned his new title, William the Conqueror.

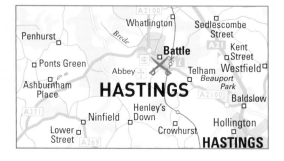

Location:
Battle, 7 miles
northwest
from the
centre of
Hastings

HAROLD

1

ENGLISH

housekarls

FLEMISH

2

2

2

NORMANS

WILLIAM

KEY

English army
Normans
Norman cavalry
viewpoint
P car park

NORTHALLERTON
22nd August 1138

1. War: Medieval Wars
2. Opposing forces: English/Scots
3. Opposing commanders: Thurstan, Archbishop of York/King David I
4. Strength of opposing forces: Not recorded
5. Number of casualties: Not recorded
6. Outcome: English victory
7. Consequences: With this victory King Stephen postponed rebellion and civil war, though not for long

England Photographic Atlas: Page 678, D1

When Henry I died suddenly in 1135, he left the English crown to his daughter Matilda. However, with the backing of the citizens of London and most of the barons, Matilda's second cousin Stephen laid claim to the throne, despite his earlier oath of fealty to Matilda. Matilda's claim was championed by her uncle, King David of Scotland, who was not acting entirely in his niece's interest – he was also hoping to annex Northumberland for Scotland.

After three years of cross-border raids, David began a determined assault on northern England in July 1138. King Stephen's forces were employed quelling rebellions in the south, and it was Thurstan, Archbishop of York, who defended the north. The Archbishop succeeded in raising an army by declaring that the campaign was a crusade with rewards in heaven, and his forces met the Scots at Northallerton on 22nd August. The English were drawn up in a single division on a gentle rise (1), facing the Scots across a slight dip in the terrain (2). The Scots' first charge was made by the unarmoured men of Galloway (3) who fought determinedly but failed to break the English line. Prince Henry then led a cavalry charge from the Scottish right flank (4) which carried him right through the English ranks but proved ineffective because it was unsupported by the Scottish infantry. Legend has it that an Englishman then picked up a head from the field, held it aloft and shouted King David was killed. At this the Scots turned and fled, giving victory to Thurstan, who fought under the standard of the Yorkshire saints.

KEY

Scottish army

Scottish cavalry

English army

English cavalry

viewpoint

monument

Hutton Bonville
Streetlam
Danby Wiske
Oaktree Hill
East Harlsey
NORTHALLERTON
Great Langton
Brompton
A167
Kirby Sigston
Cod Beck
Yafforth
A684
Thrintoft
Romanby
Northallerton

Location:
2 miles north
from the
centre of
Northallerton

SCOTS

KING DAVID

Standard Hill

2

GALWEGIANS

PRINCE
HENRY

3

1

THURSTAN

4

ENGLISH

LEWES
14th May 1264

1. War: Medieval Wars
2. Opposing forces: Rebel barons/Royalists
3. Opposing commanders: Simon de Montfort/King Henry III
4. Strength of opposing forces: 5,000 Rebels/10,000 Royalists
5. Number of casualties: 1,300/2,700 (disputed)
6. Outcome: Rebel victory
7. Consequences: For a year de Montfort governed England in the King's name

England Photographic Atlas: Page 148, E6

Henry III was an extremely cultured sovereign, but he was also one who believed in the absolute power of the monarch. This, together with the huge tax burden caused by the rebuilding of Westminster Abbey and by Henry's acceptance of the crown of Sicily for his son Edmund, led to his being forced to accept demands for reform as laid down in the Provisions of Oxford in 1258. When Henry reneged on the Provisions six years later, Simon de Montfort, the Earl of Leicester, called the barons to arms.

Early on the morning of 14th May 1264, de Montfort's forces marched eight miles from their camp at Fletching to Lewes, where the royal army was billetted. De Montfort drew up his forces on Offham Hill (1) and almost immediately Prince Edward, without waiting for the rest of the royal army to assemble, launched an impulsive cavalry attack (2) which scattered de Montfort's left wing (3). The King, whose troops had camped further south and had only just deployed themselves, was now forced to follow up this attack with an infantry charge on de Montfort's line (4), up the hill and without the support of the Prince's cavalry which had left the field in pursuit of the rebel left. First Cornwall's troops and then the King's were forced back down the hill and into Lewes (5), where street-fighting led to a Royalist surrender.

The terms of the surrender, known as the mise of Lewes, saw Prince Edward held hostage as a guarantor of Henry's good behaviour and left de Montfort in control of the King. With de Montfort's famous parliament called the following year, the Battle of Lewes became a significant step on the road to British democracy.

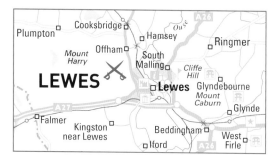

Location:
1 mile north-
west from the
centre of
Lewes

KEY

Royal army

Baronial army

◄ viewpoint

P car park

River Ouse

L E W E S

5

Castle

EVESHAM
4th August 1265

1. War: Medieval Wars
2. Opposing forces: Rebel barons/Royalists
3. Opposing commanders: Simon de Montfort/Prince Edward
4. Strength of opposing forces: 6,000 Rebels/8,000 Royalists
5. Number of casualties: 3-4,000 Rebels
6. Outcome: Royalist victory
7. Consequences: Edward suppressed de Montfort's rebellion and restored the power of the Crown

England Photographic Atlas: Page 390, A1

After his victory at Lewes (p. 26), Simon de Montfort had promised "government by consent" but he discovered that maintaining power was not quite so simple. Many of his supporters became disillusioned with his methods and defected to the royalist cause, most significantly the Earl of Gloucester, and in the meantime Prince Edward managed to escape from his gaolers by challenging them to a horse race – having won the race, he simply carried on riding away from Hereford Castle where he had been held. Edward then allied himself with the Earl of Gloucester and together they raised an army to restore the authority of the crown.

Edward first attacked the camp of de Montfort's son (also Simon) at Kenilworth, destroying the rebel reinforcements, and then marched overnight to intercept the older de Montfort at Evesham, where he trapped the rebel forces in a loop of the River Avon. Edward despatched Roger Mortimer's cavalry to hold Bengeworth Bridge (1), de Montfort's only escape to the south, and then took up position with the Duke of Gloucester on Green Hill to the north (2), leaving de Montfort no choice but to fight his way out. De Montfort's only option was to form his army into a single column and attempt to charge through the gap between Gloucester's and the Prince's troops (3) but the royalist cavalry simply closed on the rebel flanks (4) and butchered between three and four thousand of the rebel troops including de Montfort himself.

The Chronicle of Robert of Gloucester describes the engagement as murder, "for battle none it was", and yet, despite the overwhelming outcome, the barons still refused to accept defeat. Final reconciliation came in 1275, when Edward himself (as Edward I), enshrined parts of the Provisions of Oxford in the Statue of Westminster.

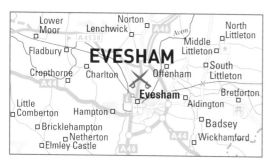

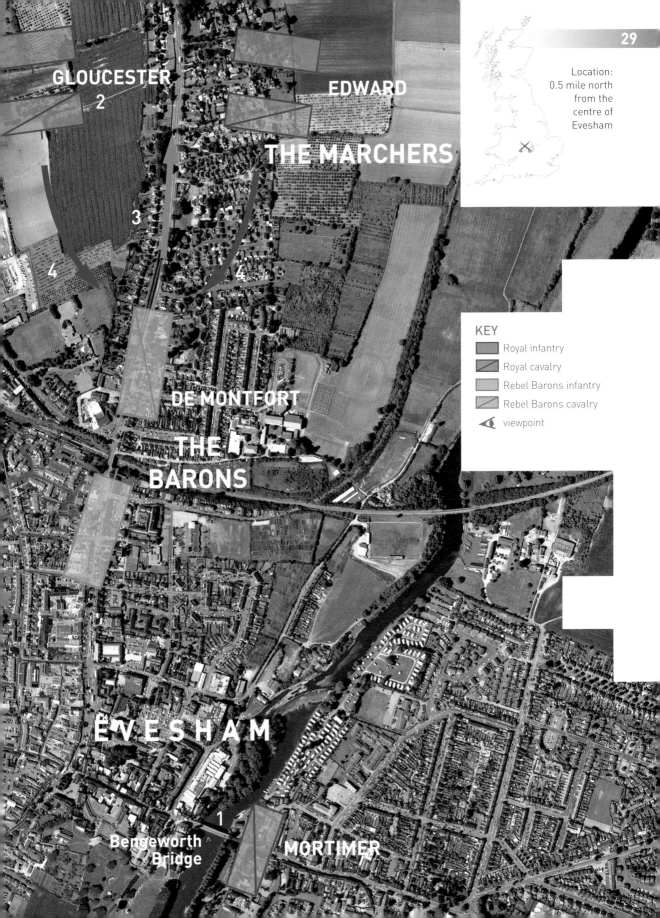

Location:
0.5 mile north
from the
centre of
Evesham

GLOUCESTER
2

EDWARD

THE MARCHERS

3

4

4

DE MONTFORT

THE
BARONS

KEY
Royal infantry
Royal cavalry
Rebel Barons infantry
Rebel Barons cavalry
viewpoint

EVESHAM

1

Bengeworth
Bridge

MORTIMER

BANNOCKBURN
23rd and 24th June 1314

1. War: Scottish Wars of Independence
2. Opposing forces: English/Scots
3. Opposing commanders: King Edward II/Robert Bruce
4. Strength of opposing forces: Disputed
5. Number of casualties: Disputed
6. Outcome: Scottish victory
7. Consequences: Reaffirmed the independence of Scotland

After the betrayal of William Wallace to the English in 1305, Scottish resistance to Edward I seemed to have been beaten. But with the erstwhile King John Balliol exiled in France, having relinquished power to Edward I in 1296, other claimants to the Scottish throne stepped forward. Robert Bruce killed his rival John Comyn in 1306 and within a month had been crowned King of Scotland.

Bruce then proceeded to wage a guerrilla war which eroded much of the English power in Scotland but was forced into a direct confrontation with a much larger army when Edward II marched north to relieve Stirling Castle. Bruce prepared for battle at Bannockburn, two miles southeast of Stirling, digging pits to protect his army from English cavalry charges. Edward divided his forces as he approached, hoping that one contingent would drive the Scots into an unexpected flanking attack by the other, but both suffered badly in preliminary encounters with the Scots on 23rd June, encouraging Bruce to take the initiative the following day.

The dispirited English camped overnight between the River Forth and the Bannock Burn (1), and as dawn broke Edward was amazed to see the numerically inferior Scottish force advancing towards him (2). The English knights underestimated the Scots and, not bothering to form up properly, attacked piecemeal. This lack of discipline, together with Edward II's weak leadership, meant that the Scots gained the upper hand in close fighting and the English were put to flight. As a result Robert Bruce was popularly proclaimed King of Scotland, but Scottish sovereignty was not recognized by the English until Edward III signed the Treaty of Northampton in 1328.

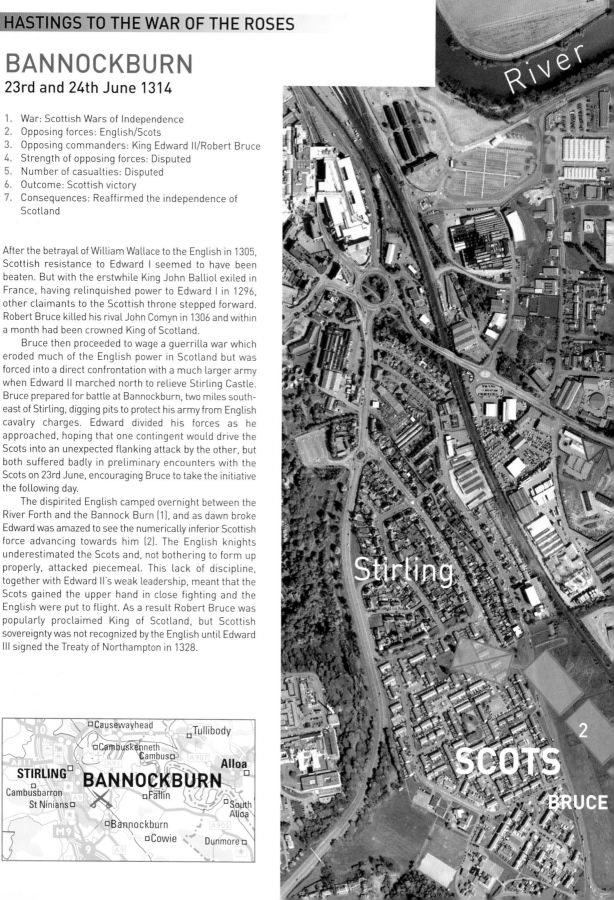

Forth

ENGLISH

EDWARD

1

KEY

- English infantry
- English cavalry
- ▲▲▲ English archers
- Scottish infantry
- Scottish cavalry

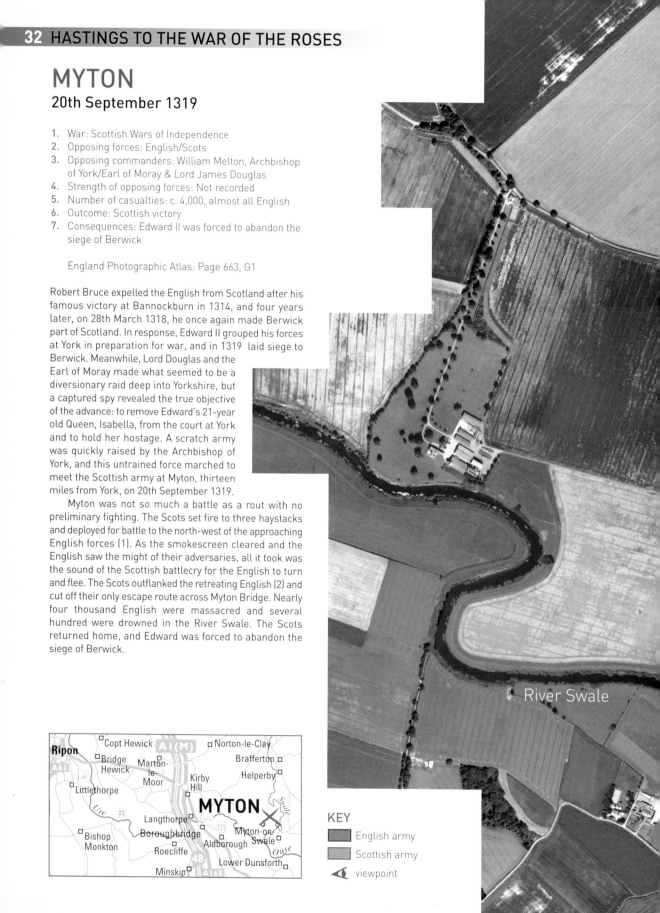

MYTON
20th September 1319

1. War: Scottish Wars of Independence
2. Opposing forces: English/Scots
3. Opposing commanders: William Melton, Archbishop of York/Earl of Moray & Lord James Douglas
4. Strength of opposing forces: Not recorded
5. Number of casualties: c. 4,000, almost all English
6. Outcome: Scottish victory
7. Consequences: Edward II was forced to abandon the siege of Berwick

England Photographic Atlas: Page 663, G1

Robert Bruce expelled the English from Scotland after his famous victory at Bannockburn in 1314, and four years later, on 28th March 1318, he once again made Berwick part of Scotland. In response, Edward II grouped his forces at York in preparation for war, and in 1319 laid siege to Berwick. Meanwhile, Lord Douglas and the Earl of Moray made what seemed to be a diversionary raid deep into Yorkshire, but a captured spy revealed the true objective of the advance: to remove Edward's 21-year old Queen, Isabella, from the court at York and to hold her hostage. A scratch army was quickly raised by the Archbishop of York, and this untrained force marched to meet the Scottish army at Myton, thirteen miles from York, on 20th September 1319.

Myton was not so much a battle as a rout with no preliminary fighting. The Scots set fire to three haystacks and deployed for battle to the north-west of the approaching English forces (1). As the smokescreen cleared and the English saw the might of their adversaries, all it took was the sound of the Scottish battlecry for the English to turn and flee. The Scots outflanked the retreating English (2) and cut off their only escape route across Myton Bridge. Nearly four thousand English were massacred and several hundred were drowned in the River Swale. The Scots returned home, and Edward was forced to abandon the siege of Berwick.

River Swale

KEY
English army
Scottish army
viewpoint

Location:
11 miles
southeast
from the
centre of
Ripon

DOUGLAS
&
MORAY

2

1

MELTON

2

BOROUGHBRIDGE
16th March 1322

1. War: Medieval Wars
2. Opposing forces: Rebels/Royalists
3. Opposing commanders: Thomas, Earl of Lancaster/Sir Andrew de Harcla
4. Strength of opposing forces: 3,000 Rebels/4,000 Royalists
5. Number of casualties: Not recorded
6. Outcome: Royalist victory
7. Consequences: The rebellion was crushed and Lancaster executed for treason

England Photographic Atlas: Page 663, F1

As well as being unsuccessful in Scotland (see Bannockburn, p. 30), Edward II had continuous problems to deal with in his own realm, both from rebellious barons and from his treacherous wife Isabella, "the she-wolf of France". The Earls of Lancaster and Hereford attempted a rebellion but timed it badly, failing to gain the support of the other nobles: having succumbed to the royal forces at Burton-on-Trent they retreated through Yorkshire hoping to join forces with the Scots. On 16th March 1322 they found the Sheriff of Cumberland, Sir Andrew de Harcla, blocking their way at the crossing of the River Ure in Boroughbridge.

De Harcla placed pikemen and knights on the northern side of the bridge (1), with the remainder of his force in a "schiltron" (a defensive block pioneered by William Wallace) on the northern side of a ford to the east of the bridge (2). Lancaster divided his forces, leaving Hereford to storm the bridge on foot (3) while he attempted to lead his cavalry across the ford (4). Hereford was killed at the bridge – which held firm – while Lancaster found he could not even enter the water for the number of arrows despatched by de Harcla's archers. An overnight truce was called but the following morning Lancaster found that most of his surviving forces had deserted him and he was forced to surrender. He was confined at York Castle and eventually beheaded. The severity of this sentence may have had less to do with the rebellion than the fact that Lancaster was involved in the murder of Edward's supposed lover Piers Gaveston.

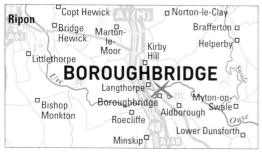

River Ure

Location:
9 miles south-
east from the
centre of
Ripon

2

4

DE HARCLA

1
Boroughbridge

3

LANCASTER

HEREFORD

P

KEY

Royalists
Rebels
viewpoint
P car park

HALIDON HILL
19th July 1333

1. War: Medieval Wars
2. Opposing forces: English/Scots
3. Opposing commanders: King Edward III & Edward Balliol/Sir Archibald Douglas
4. Strength of opposing forces: 10,000 English/c. 15,000 Scots
5. Number of casualties: c. 100 English/estimates vary from 4,000–10,000 Scots
6. Outcome: English victory
7. Consequences: Balliol was reinstated as King of Scotland, and Berwick-upon-Tweed once again became part of England

England Photographic Atlas: Page 746, D3

Robert Bruce died in 1329, and the Scottish throne passed to his five-year old son David. This shift in the balance of power encouraged the exiled Edward Balliol, (son of John Balliol who had reigned from 1292–96) to retake the Scottish throne, but he was deposed after only four months and forced to fall back on the support of Edward III in England. The two Edwards crossed the Scottish border and laid siege to Berwick (which was at that time a Scottish town) in May 1333. Sir Archibald Douglas, in charge of the Scottish Royal army, attempted to draw the English forces away from the siege with a series of raids on the border country, but to no avail: eventually he was forced to confront the English in a pitched battle on 19th July 1333.

The English forces were deployed in three divisions on the high ground of Halidon Hill (1) to the north-west of Berwick, with the king commanding the centre. The Scots found that they could not cross the boggy approach to the foot of the hill on horseback and had to approach on foot (2) before advancing up the slope towards the English (3). With the advantage of high ground protected by a bog, the English archers were more than a match for the Scots scrambling up the hill towards them, and the Scottish attack soon turned into a rout, with one estimate of English losses as low as 14 men. It is said that the Scots lost six earls, "70 barons, 500 knights and spearmen uncountable" as well as Sir Archibald Douglas himself. Berwick fell to the English and Balliol was installed on the Scottish throne as a puppet for Edward III.

2
STEWART

MORAY

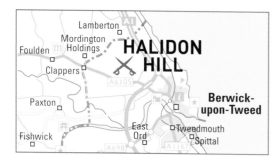

HALIDON HILL

Lamberton
Mordington
Holdings
Foulden
Clappers
A6105
Paxton
Berwick-upon-Tweed
East Ord
Tweedmouth
Fishwick
Spittal

KEY

English army

Scottish army

◀ viewpoint

P car park

monument

37

Location:
2 miles north-
west from the
centre of
Berwick-
upon-
Tweed

DOUGLAS

Halidon Hill

3

1

P

EDWARD

BALLIOL

NEVILLE'S CROSS
17th October 1346

1. War: Medieval Wars
2. Opposing forces: English/Scots
3. Opposing commanders: Neville, Percy & Archbishop of York/King David II
4. Strength of opposing forces: 10,700 English/15,000 Scots
5. Number of casualties: 1,000 Scots
6. Outcome: English victory
7. Consequences: King David was captured and imprisoned until 1357

England Photographic Atlas: Page 709, E2

Edward III's claim to the French throne through his mother Isabella, daughter of Philip III, was unrecognized in France but Edward nonetheless began the so-called Hundred Years War in pursuit of the French crown. Edward defeated the French at Crecy on 26th August 1346, whereupon Philip VI of France appealed to his ally David II of Scotland to divert Edward's attention and resources. David accordingly raised an army to invade England, also hoping to regain some of the Scottish lands ceded to England by Edward Balliol, grandson of the deposed puppet king John Balliol.

Edward had anticipated such a move, and had therefore appointed the Archbishop of York, with Sir Ralph Neville and Sir Henry Percy, to defend northern England. The Scots had made it as far south as Durham, plundering as they went, when a raiding party was surprised at Merrington and routed by the English force. The English then deployed themselves on a ridge near Neville's Cross (1) and waited for King David to advance to meet them. The English had chosen their ground well. As the Scots advanced they were forced by a ravine to bunch in the centre (2), providing an easy target for the English archers. The Scottish right and left were both forced back by English cavalry charges (3), leaving the King's troop exposed in the centre. When they, too, eventually retreated, the Scottish king was captured and afterwards imprisoned in the Tower of London.

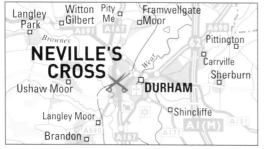

SCOTS

DAVID

ROBERT

Location:
0.5 mile west
from the
centre of
Durham

2

3

ROKEBY

NEVILLE

PERCY

1

DURHAM

ENGLISH

KEY

◢◣ English infantry

◢◣ English cavalry

▲▲▲ English archers

◢◣ Scottish infantry

◀ viewpoint

OTTERBURN
19th August 1388

1. War: Medieval Wars
2. Opposing forces: English/Scots
3. Opposing commanders: Sir Henry Percy & Sir Ralph Percy/James, 2nd Earl of Douglas
4. Strength of opposing forces: 7-8,000 English/6-7,000 Scots
5. Number of casualties: Not recorded
6. Outcome: Scottish victory
7. Consequences: James Douglas was killed and both Percys taken prisoner

England Photographic Atlas: Page 739, G6

Border warfare between England and Scotland continued throughout the 14th century, with the house of Percy, Earls of Northumberland, always first in line to suffer from Scottish raiding parties. In summer 1388 Sir Archibald Douglas and James, 2nd Earl of Douglas, led a two-pronged attack across the border, one party striking westwards towards Carlisle and the other, under James, penetrating as far as Durham. This party was pursued by the Earl of Northumberland's sons Henry and Ralph Percy and in a skirmish near Newcastle Douglas captured Henry Percy's lance pennon. Henry was restrained from making an immediate attempt to recover the pennon, but swore to regain it before the Scots reached the border. He caught up with Douglas at Otterburn on the night of 19th August.

Percy resolved to act immediately, despite the lateness of the hour. Douglas was camped beside the River Rede, with rising ground to the north (1). Percy sent Sir Thomas Umfraville on an outflanking march round the camp, while he himself approached from the east (2). Douglas quickly formed his men into two divisions, sending one forward to meet the Percys (3) and taking the other on a slightly circuitous route to approach the English right flank on the downhill slope (4). The Scots succeeded in forcing the English downhill towards the river, keeping them on the run despite the loss of Douglas to three spears. Both Percys were captured, unsupported by Umfraville, who had overcome the camp guard and then withdrawn, taking no further part in the battle.

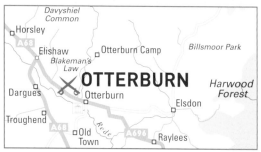

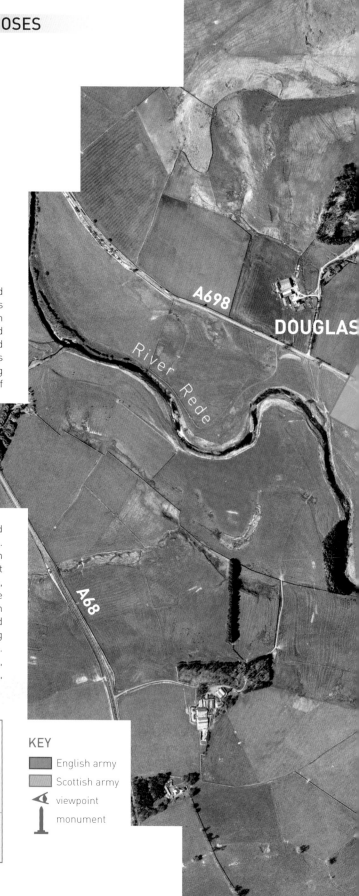

KEY

- English army
- Scottish army
- viewpoint
- monument

Location:
31 miles
northwest
from the
centre of
Newcastle

2

Cattle & camp
followers

4

3   1

2

PERCY

Otterburn

Albright Hussey

PRINCE HENRY

SHREWSBURY
21st July 1403

1. War: Medieval Wars
2. Opposing forces: Rebels/Royalists
3. Opposing commanders:
   Sir Henry Percy (Hotspur)/King Henry IV
4. Strength of opposing forces: Estimates vary widely
5. Number of casualties: 3,000 rebels /3,000 royalists
6. Outcome: Royalist victory
7. Consequences: Henry Percy was killed and Henry IV consolidated his position as usurper of the throne

England Photographic Atlas: Page 475, E2

When Henry Bolingbroke deposed Richard II in 1399 to become King Henry IV, the main champions of his cause had been the Percys of Northumberland. However, the Percys were aggrieved that after the Battle of Homildon Hill Henry had broken with tradition, failing to allow them to collect the ransom for their prisoners and insisting instead that the prisoners be handed over to the King. Henry added insult to injury by refusing to provide a ransom for Sir Henry Percy's brother-in-law, and so the Percys rebelled, forging an alliance with Owain Glyndwr.

When he heard news of this rebellion, Henry was already marching northwards to lend support to the Percys against another Scottish incursion, and diverted his forces eastwards to intercept Henry Percy at Shrewsbury before he could link up with the forces commanded by his father and Glyndwr. Percy deployed his forces in a single division on a ridge known today as "Battlefield" (1), and on the morning of 21st July 1401 Henry rode out to meet them, his forces deployed in two divisions, one commanded by the king himself and the other by his son Prince Henry (later Henry V). After an exchange of arrows, Henry's division moved forward, only to be repelled by Percy and the Earl of Douglas (2). (Douglas was now fighting for the Percys instead of against them as he had done at Otterburn [p. 40]. However, this rebel success was short-lived, because in the meantime Prince Henry had ridden straight through the rebel right flank and then turned, trapping the rebels between the two royal divisions (3). Percy was killed in the melee and, hearing the news, his supporters fled the field.

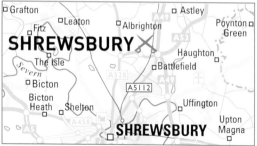

KEY

▬ Royalist infantry

▲▲▲ Royalist archers

▬ Rebel infantry

◀ viewpoint

P car park

REBELS

HOTSPUR

1

Location:
2 miles north
from the
centre of
Shrewsbury

2

KING HENRY

ROYALISTS

A49

A53

P

WARS OF THE ROSES AND THE SCOTTISH WARS

ST ALBANS
22nd May 1455

1. War: Wars of the Roses
2. Opposing forces: Lancastrians/Yorkists
3. Opposing commanders: King Henry VI/Richard, Duke of York
4. Strength of opposing forces: 2-3,000 Lancastrians/3,000 Yorkists
5. Number of casualties: Not recorded
6. Outcome: Yorkist victory
7. Consequences: The skirmish proved to be the preamble to 32 years of plots, rebellions and battles that later became known as the Wars of the Roses

England Photographic Atlas: Page 280, B4

Henry VI suffered a mental breakdown during 1453, and his cousin Richard, Duke of York (who had a rival claim to the throne dating back to the death of Richard II), manoeuvred himself into the role of Protector of England. This led to a power struggle between York and the King's favourite the Duke of Somerset: Somerset had been instrumental in suppressing an earlier uprising by York, and now found himself imprisoned in the Tower. When Henry regained his faculties, Somerset was freed from the Tower and York, fearing retribution, prepared to defend himself against his rival.

Having amassed an army, York marched southwards, demanding the removal of Somerset, while Henry and Somerset marched northwards. On 21st May the King's forces reached St Albans and prepared the town for defence – York arrived later the same day and set up camp in Key Field to the east of the town. Henry refused York's demands that Somerset be dismissed, so on the morning of 22nd May York, determined to remove Somerset personally, launched an attack on the eastern boundary of the town, probably in two divisions at the north and south of the main street (1 & 2). These attacks were repelled and eventually the Earl of Warwick broke through in the centre (3), leading to hand-to-hand fighting in the market-place during which Somerset was killed and the King captured. Having deposed his rival, York escorted the King to London and swore his allegiance. Henry diplomatically gave Somerset's title of Constable of England to York, ensuring peace for the next four years.

A second battle took place at St Albans on 17th February 1461, when Queen Margaret stormed the town and released King Henry, who was being held captive there by the Earl of Warwick.

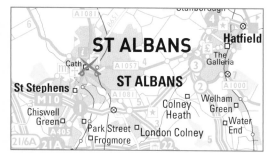

HENRY & BUCKINGHAM

Abbey

CLIFFORD

KEY

Yorkist army

Lancastrian army

Location:
St Albans town
centre

SOMERSET

Lancastrian defences

YORK

1

WARWICK

3

SALISBURY

2

BLORE HEATH
23rd September 1459

1. War: Wars of the Roses
2. Opposing forces: Lancastrians/Yorkists
3. Opposing commanders: Lord Audley/Earl of Salisbury
4. Strength of opposing forces: 10,000 Lancastrians/5,000 Yorkists
5. Number of casualties: 2,000 Lancastrians
6. Outcome: Yorkist victory
7. Consequences: Audley failed to prevent Salisbury's forces from joining the main Yorkist army at Ludlow

England Photographic Atlas: Page 490, E3

Four years of uneasy peace after the Battle of St Albans were broken when, in spring 1459, Queen Margaret issued indictments for treason against the Duke of York and the Earl of Warwick, forcing them to take up arms. The Earl of Salisbury (Warwick's father) was moving his forces southwards to join the Duke of York at Ludlow when he was intercepted at Blore Heath by the Prince of Wales's army under the command of Lord Audley.

Salisbury found his way blocked by a force almost twice the size of his own, deployed on a shallow ridge to the east of what is now called Hempmill Brook (1). Realising that either withdrawal or attack would be disastrous, Salisbury made the best of his defences, deploying his forces with the wood protecting the left flank (2) and drawing up his wagons to protect the right. He then feigned retreat in order to provoke an attack by Audley, who attempted three separate assaults across the brook, each of them repelled by the Yorkist archers. Audley was killed in the third assault, at which point his demoralised forces withdrew from the field and were pursued by the Yorkists to the banks of the River Tern. Audley had failed to deliver Salisbury to the Queen, and Salisbury's forces were now able to continue to their rendezvous at Ludlow.

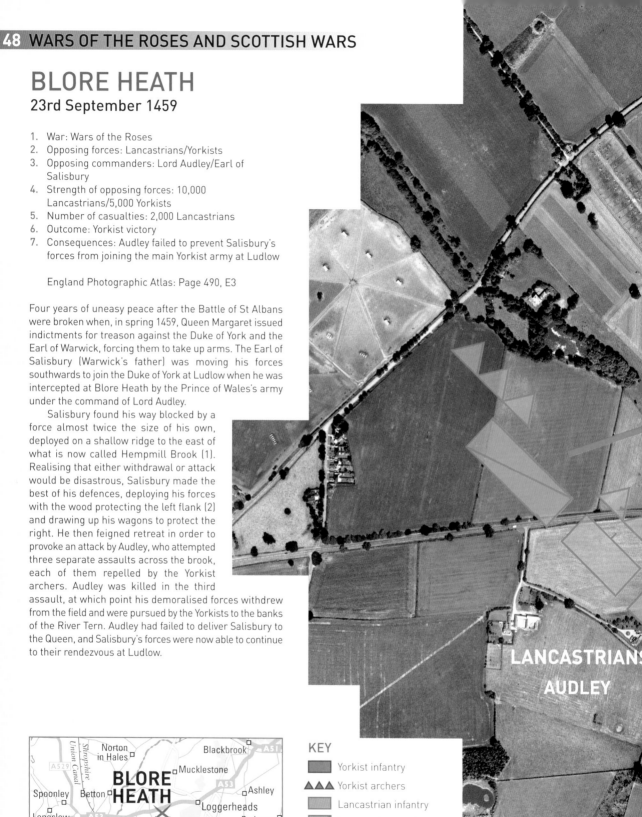

LANCASTRIANS
AUDLEY

KEY

▮ Yorkist infantry
▲▲▲ Yorkist archers
▨ Lancastrian infantry
▧ Lancastrian cavalry
▲▲▲ Lancastrian archers
⚐ viewpoint
☗ monument

49

Location:
4 miles east
from the
centre of
Market
Drayton

A53

YORKISTS

SALISBURY

1

2

Blore

NORTHAMPTON
10th July 1460

1. War: Wars of the Roses
2. Opposing forces: Lancastrians/Yorkists
3. Opposing commanders: Duke of Buckingham/Earl of March & Earl of Warwick
4. Strength of opposing forces: 5,000 Lancastrians/7,000 Yorkists
5. Number of casualties: Not recorded
6. Outcome: Yorkist victory
7. Consequences: The Act of Settlement was passed, making the Duke of York heir to the throne in place of the Prince of Wales

England Photographic Atlas: Page 413, G1

Lancastrian defeat at Blore Heath (p. 48) was followed three weeks later by a Yorkist retreat before the King's forces near Worcester. After their ignominious retreat, the Yorkist leadership fled abroad, York to Ireland and the Earls of March, Salisbury and Warwick to Calais. A failed Lancastrian raid on Calais encouraged the Yorkists to launch a counter-strike against Sandwich, establishing a garrison there and then taking London. Meanwhile, Henry VI was in the Midlands, raising an army to defend against an expected invasion from Ireland by the Duke of York. Without waiting for York's forces to land, March and Warwick moved northwards to confront the king before the royal army reached full strength.

The Yorkists had the numerical superiority but when they met the royal forces outside Northampton, they found that the Lancastrians had dug themselves in to a heavily fortified position to the south of the River Nene (1) and were protected by heavy cannon. However, treachery and the weather won the day for the Yorkists: heavy rain had soaked the Lancastrians' gunpowder, rendering the cannon useless, and when March led his forces towards the Lancastrian defences (2), he was given entry to their fortifications by Lord Grey of Ruthyn. The Lancastrians now found themselves trapped within the walls and quickly succumbed, with Buckingham killed and the king himself captured.

York now pressed his claim to the throne, and on 10th October 1460 the Act of Settlement was passed, making York the heir to the throne in place of the Prince of Wales. Queen Margaret would not accept this, and immediately began to raise an army to defend the Lancastrian inheritance of the crown.

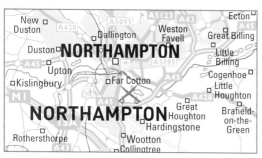

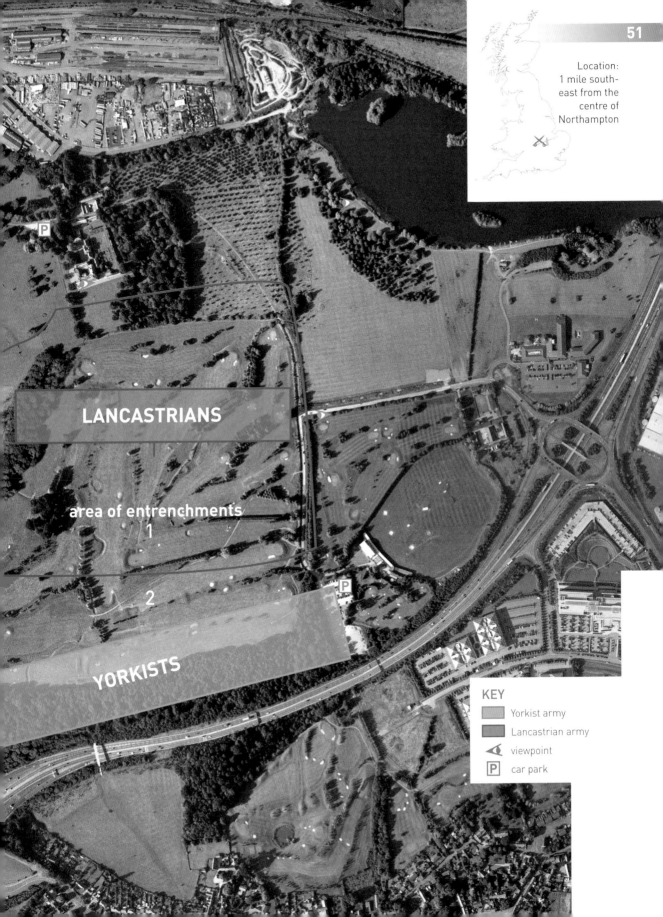

Location:
1 mile south-
east from the
centre of
Northampton

LANCASTRIANS

area of entrenchments

1

2

YORKISTS

KEY
Yorkist army
Lancastrian army
viewpoint
car park

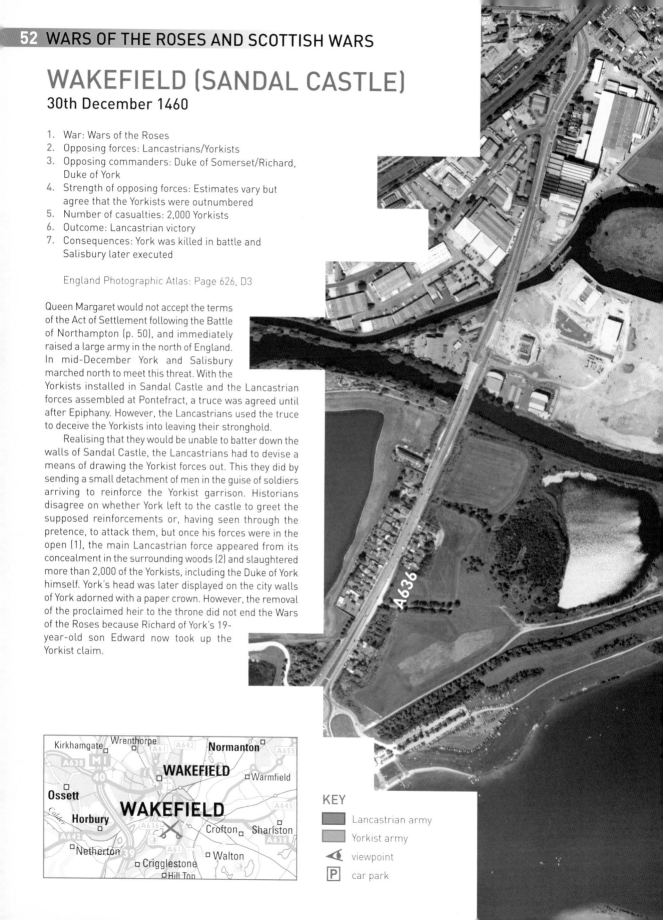

WAKEFIELD (SANDAL CASTLE)
30th December 1460

1. War: Wars of the Roses
2. Opposing forces: Lancastrians/Yorkists
3. Opposing commanders: Duke of Somerset/Richard, Duke of York
4. Strength of opposing forces: Estimates vary but agree that the Yorkists were outnumbered
5. Number of casualties: 2,000 Yorkists
6. Outcome: Lancastrian victory
7. Consequences: York was killed in battle and Salisbury later executed

England Photographic Atlas: Page 626, D3

Queen Margaret would not accept the terms of the Act of Settlement following the Battle of Northampton (p. 50), and immediately raised a large army in the north of England. In mid-December York and Salisbury marched north to meet this threat. With the Yorkists installed in Sandal Castle and the Lancastrian forces assembled at Pontefract, a truce was agreed until after Epiphany. However, the Lancastrians used the truce to deceive the Yorkists into leaving their stronghold.

Realising that they would be unable to batter down the walls of Sandal Castle, the Lancastrians had to devise a means of drawing the Yorkist forces out. This they did by sending a small detachment of men in the guise of soldiers arriving to reinforce the Yorkist garrison. Historians disagree on whether York left to the castle to greet the supposed reinforcements or, having seen through the pretence, to attack them, but once his forces were in the open (1), the main Lancastrian force appeared from its concealment in the surrounding woods (2) and slaughtered more than 2,000 of the Yorkists, including the Duke of York himself. York's head was later displayed on the city walls of York adorned with a paper crown. However, the removal of the proclaimed heir to the throne did not end the Wars of the Roses because Richard of York's 19-year-old son Edward now took up the Yorkist claim.

KEY

Lancastrian army

Yorkist army

◄ viewpoint

P car park

River Calder

Portobello

previously woodland

CLIFFORD

2

2

ROSSE

YORK

1

previously woodland

2

WILTSHIRE

Sandal Castle

Sandal Magna

P

TOWTON
29th March 1461

1. War: Wars of the Roses
2. Opposing forces: Lancastrians/Yorkists
3. Opposing commanders: Duke of Somerset/Edward, Duke of York (proclaimed King Edward IV)
4. Strength of opposing forces: 30,000 Lancastrians/30,000 Yorkists
5. Number of casualties: 20,000 Lancastrians/8,000 Yorkists
6. Outcome: Yorkist victory
7. Consequences: Henry VI and Queen Margaret fled to Scotland and York was crowned Edward IV

England Photographic Atlas: Page 648, A1

After the death of Richard, Duke of York, at the Battle of Wakefield (p. 52), his son Edward was victorious at Mortimer's Cross (2nd February 1461) and marched to London, where the nobles proclaimed him King Edward IV on 4th March. But in the meantime, Queen Margaret's Lancastrian forces had defeated the Earl of Warwick at the Second Battle of St Albans (17th February 1461) and succeeded in freeing Henry VI. Both kings knew that their claim to the throne would be decided in battle, and their two armies met on 29th March 1461 at Towton.

The Duke of Somerset had drawn up the Lancastrian forces on a ridge between Towton and Saxton (1) with a small ambush party concealed in woods to the south west. The Yorkists were deployed to the south of the Lancastrian line (2) and began the battle with a ruse that took advantage of a blinding snowstorm: Lord Fauconberg ordered his archers to let fly a single volley of arrows and then withdraw. Unable to see what was happening, the Lancastrians spent their arrows shooting into the wind before the Yorkists retrieved their enemies' arrows and began to shoot in earnest. The Lancastrian right then advanced under the Duke of Somerset (3), but the Lancastrian left failed to support this assault and the Yorkist line stood firm. With the arrival of Yorkist reinforcements under the Duke of Norfolk (4), who attacked the Lancastrian left flank, the battle turned in Edward IV's favour and the Lancastrians were routed.

Despite all the bloodshed and a resounding Yorkist victory, nothing was resolved by the Battle of Towton. Edward IV had proved his claim in battle and was duly crowned in June, but Henry VI had made his escape northwards. England still had two kings and the Wars of the Roses continued.

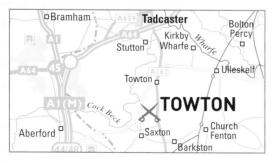

Cock Beck

Castle Hill Wood

KEY

Lancastrian army

Yorkist army

◀ viewpoint

P car park

monument

Location:
4 miles south
from the
centre of
Tadcaster

Towton

A162

LANCASTRIANS

1

SOMERSET
3

EDWARD 2

YORKISTS

NORFOLK

4

Saxton

BARNET
14th April 1471

1. War: Wars of the Roses
2. Opposing forces: Lancastrians/Yorkists
3. Opposing commanders: Earl of Warwick/King Edward IV
4. Strength of opposing forces: 15,000 Lancastrians/10,000 Yorkists
5. Number of casualties: 1,000 Lancastrians/500 Yorkists
6. Outcome: Yorkist victory
7. Consequences: Edward crushed his former ally Warwick, who was killed in the battle, leaving Queen Margaret as Edward's only remaining adversary fighting for Henry VI's cause

England Photographic Atlas: Page 261, F2

Although the Lancastrian position was precarious in the ten years after defeat at the Battle of Towton (p. 54), the Earl of Warwick exploited discontent in the Yorkist ranks to provoke various uprisings and in 1470 forced Edward IV to withdraw to France. Warwick then released Henry VI from the Tower and restored him to the throne. Edward returned to England in 1471 with support from his French ally Charles the Bold and reoccupied London. Warwick marched southwards, hoping to overcome the royal forces while Edward was preoccupied with retaking the capital, but Edward surprised Warwick with the speed of his manoeuvres, and was ready to do battle when the two armies met at Barnet on the night of 13th April 1471.

Edward deployed his forces in three divisions (1) ready to launch a dawn attack on the Lancastrian position (2), but deployment in darkness coupled with an advance through the dawn mist meant that the Yorkist right overlapping the Lancastrian left and vice versa. Lord Hastings, on the Yorkist left, advanced first but was driven back into Barnet by the Earl of Oxford's men on the Lancastrian right (3). The Duke of Gloucester, commanding the Yorkist right, advanced, but missed the enemy because of the overlap and turned to make a flanking attack (4) which began to overcome the Lancastrians in hand-to-hand fighting. In the meantime, Oxford rejoined the battle from the south (the direction of the Yorkist position) and was mistakenly fired on by Somerset's men, which led to cries of treason and the collapse of Lancastrian morale. With impeccable timing, Edward launched his reserve into the fray and forced the Lancastrians to flee. Warwick was killed in the Lancastrian retreat, and Edward's only remaining adversary was Henry VI's Queen Margaret.

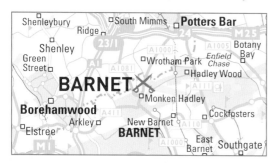

Location:
0.5 mile north
from the
centre of
Barnet

LANCASTRIANS

WARWICK

SOMERSET

2

EXETER

A1000

4

KEY

Yorkist infantry
▲▲▲ Yorkist archers
Lancastrian infantry
▲▲▲ Lancastrian archers
viewpoint
monument

1

EDWARD

GLOUCESTER

YORKISTS

B A R N E T

TEWKESBURY
4th May 1471

1. War: Wars of the Roses
2. Opposing forces: Lancastrians/Yorkists
3. Opposing commanders: Duke of Somerset/King Edward IV
4. Strength of opposing forces: 6,000 Lancastrians/5,000 Yorkists
5. Number of casualties: 2,000 Lancastrians
6. Outcome: Yorkist victory
7. Consequences: The Prince of Wales was killed in battle, Queen Margaret captured, and afterwards Henry VI was murdered in the Tower; Edward IV never had to fight for his crown again

England Photographic Atlas: Page 388, D6

On the day that Edward IV defeated Warwick at Barnet (p. 56), Henry VI's Queen, Margaret of Anjou, landed at Weymouth to secure the Lancastrian claim to the throne. In order to link up with her ally Jasper Tudor in Wales, Margaret had to cross the Severn, but was prevented from doing so by Yorkist supporters at Gloucester and was therefore forced to march on to Tewkesbury where, with Edward's forces only three miles behind, the Duke of Somerset decided to make a stand.

The Lancastrians deployed in three divisions in a strong position on a hill close to Tewkesbury Abbey (1). On the morning of 4th May, Edward drew up his forces to face them (2) and deployed a small contingent of 200 spearmen in the trees on his left flank (3). After an exchange of artillery and archery fire, the Duke of Somerset, commanding the Lancastrian forces from the right flank, advanced against the Yorkist left (4) but engaged too close to the centre of the Yorkist line. Lord Wenlock (who had previously fought for the Yorkist cause) failed to support Somerset, allowing Edward's forces to turn and attack Somerset's left flank (5), and when the concealed spearmen attacked Somerset's right flank all resistance crumbled.

The remainder of the Lancastrian forces were put to flight, during which the Prince of Wales was killed and Margaret of Anjou captured. Somerset was executed two days later and Henry VI, who had been kept alive in the Tower simply to weaken the Prince of Wales's claim to the throne against Edward, was executed. Edward IV never had to fight for his crown again, although the dynastic struggle continued after his death.

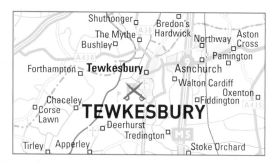

KEY

Lancastrian army

Yorkist army

viewpoint

SOMERSET

3

GLOUCESTER

Location:
0.25 miles
south from the
centre of
Tewkesbury

T E W K E S B U R Y

abbey

1

LANCASTRIANS

WENLOCK

DEVON

4

5

2

EDWARD

HASTINGS

YORKISTS

BOSWORTH
22nd August 1485

1. War: Wars of the Roses
2. Opposing forces: Lancastrians/Yorkists
3. Opposing commanders: Henry Tudor/King Richard III
4. Strength of opposing forces: 5,000 Lancastrians/8,000 Yorkists
5. Number of casualties: 200 Lancastrians/1,000 Yorkists
6. Outcome: Lancastrian victory
7. Consequences: Richard III was killed and Henry Tudor crowned Henry VII on the battlefield, beginning the Tudor dynasty

England Photographic Atlas: Page 465, H3

Tewkesbury (p. 58) was the decisive battle for Edward IV, securing the throne for the House of York. But after Edward's death in 1483, the 12 year-old Edward V and his brother Richard (the "princes in the Tower") were locked up by their uncle Richard, Duke of Gloucester, who claimed the throne as Richard III. The resulting discontent among the Yorkists paved the way for the Lancastrian Henry Tudor, exiled in France, to mount a claim for the throne, and the Wars of the Roses were reignited.

Tudor landed on 7th August 1485 and confronted the royal army at Bosworth Field on 22nd August. The Yorkist forces were already drawn up on Ambion Hill (1) and the Lancastrians were forced to deploy for battle under a storm of arrows (2). Meanwhile Lord Stanley and his brother, who were nominally supporters of the king, formed a third army on the battlefield (3) with a force of 3-4,000 men. The Duke of Norfolk charged down the hill into the Lancastrian lines (4) but this initiative was weakened by the failure of the Duke of Northumberland to support Norfolk. Meanwhile Richard's forces advanced on Henry Tudor on the Lancastrian right (5). The outcome still hung in the balance but the Stanleys, sensing victory for the Lancastrians, committed themselves on the side of Henry Tudor (6), deciding the battle in his favour.

Richard III was the last English king to be killed in battle, but whether he died fighting the treacherous Stanleys or attempting to kill Henry Tudor in personal combat, as in Shakespeare's play, is uncertain. What is certain is that after the Stanleys' intervention and Richard's death the Yorkist troops capitulated, and that Henry Tudor was crowned King Henry VII on the battlefield.

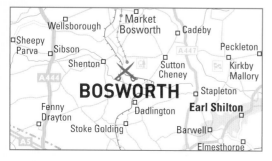

Shenton

2

OXFORD

LANCASTRIANS

HENRY

KEY

Lancastrian army

Yorkist army

Yorkist cavalry

viewpoint

car park

Location: 13 miles west from the centre of Leicester

NORFOLK

RICHARD

1

YORKISTS

NORTHUMBERLAND

4

5

Ashby-de-la-Zouch canal

6

STANLEYS

3

Dadlington

STOKE FIELD
16th June 1487

1. War: Wars of the Roses
2. Opposing forces: Tudors/Yorkists
3. Opposing commanders: King Henry VII/Earl of Lincoln & Martin Schwarz
4. Strength of opposing forces: 12,000 Royalists/8,000 Yorkists
5. Number of casualties: 2-3,000 Royalists/4,000 Yorkists
6. Outcome: Tudor victory
7. Consequences: Henry had confirmed his position as King, and Stoke marked the end of the Wars of the Roses

England Photographic Atlas: Page 516, B2

After winning the crown at Bosworth (p. 60), Henry VII imprisoned the Yorkist pretender, the Duke of Clarence, in the Tower and married Elizabeth of York, claiming that in doing so he had united the warring Roses. Despite these political moves, he still had to quash several uprisings before Yorkist supporters, led by the Earl of Lincoln, hatched a bizarre plan to raise a rebellion – they trained Lambert Simnel to impersonate Clarence, crowning him "Edward VI" in Dublin and using him as the figurehead for a Yorkist invasion. The Yorkist force comprised Irish militia and German mercenaries commanded by Martin Schwarz, and the two armies met on 16th June 1487 at Stoke Field near the village of East Stoke.

The Yorkist forces were deployed on a ridge with the River Trent protecting their right flank (1), while the Royalist forces approached from the south (2). Henry VII had fallen back and allowed the Earl of Oxford's forces to absorb the force of Lincoln and Schwarz's attack, watching from a distance as Oxford's men almost succumbed. As Henry's troops arrived in support, the lightly armed Irish fled the field, leaving the German mercenaries to fight a losing battle. Lincoln and Schwarz were both killed in the fighting and afterwards Simnel was sent to work in the royal kitchens. Stoke was the last battle Henry had to fight in defence of his crown, marking the end of the Wars of the Roses and the beginning of the Tudor dynasty.

Airfield

Location: 5 miles south-west from the centre of Newark-on-Trent

YORKISTS

LINCOLN

SCHWARZ

IRISH

East Stoke

A46

OXFORD

2

LANCASTRIANS

HENRY

River Trent

1

KEY

Lancastrian army

Yorkist army

viewpoint

FLODDEN
9th September 1513

1. War: Scottish Wars
2. Opposing forces: English/Scots
3. Opposing commanders: Earl of Surrey/King James IV
4. Strength of opposing forces: 26,000 English/35,000 Scots
5. Number of casualties: 2-4,000 English/9-10,000 Scots (estimates vary)
6. Outcome: English victory
7. Consequences: As well as 10,000 soldiers Scotland lost King James IV, twelve earls, and fourteen lords, "the flower of her nobility"

England Photographic Atlas: Page 742, B3

Where Henry VII had secured relative peace in the kingdom after the Stoke Field (p. 62), uniting the warring Roses and allying himself with James IV of Scotland through the marriage of his daughter Margaret, Henry VIII soon put that peace in jeopardy. When Henry invaded France in 1513, James IV, obliged by the terms of a mutual defence treaty to support the French, raised an army and invaded England, crossing the River Tweed at Coldstream. Henry himself was engaged in France, and had left the defence of northern England to the Earl of Surrey, who challenged the Scots to do battle on or before 9th September 1513.

Surrey was preparing for battle at Milfield on 7th September when he heard that the Scots had occupied Flodden Edge, overlooking a 500 ft drop. The English advanced to the Scottish position on the 8th but Surrey realised that to storm the Scottish position from the south would be suicidal and marched his forces to the north of the Flodden Plateau, forcing the Scots to turn around and redeploy on Branxton Hill facing north (1). King James had ordered the Scots to hold their positions and force the English to attack up the hill but, wearying of the English artillery fire, the Scottish left advanced down the hill and almost immediately dispersed the English right (2). Encouraged by this success, the two Scottish central divisions charged down the hill (3) but failed to maintain momentum and were overcome in hand to hand fighting. In the meantime, the Stanleys scaled the side of the ridge and attacked the flank of the only Scottish forces remaining on the plateau (4). Having overcome them, the Stanleys charged down the hill into the rear of King James's forces, killing the king and overcoming the last of the Scottish resistance.

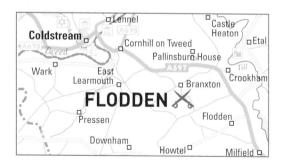

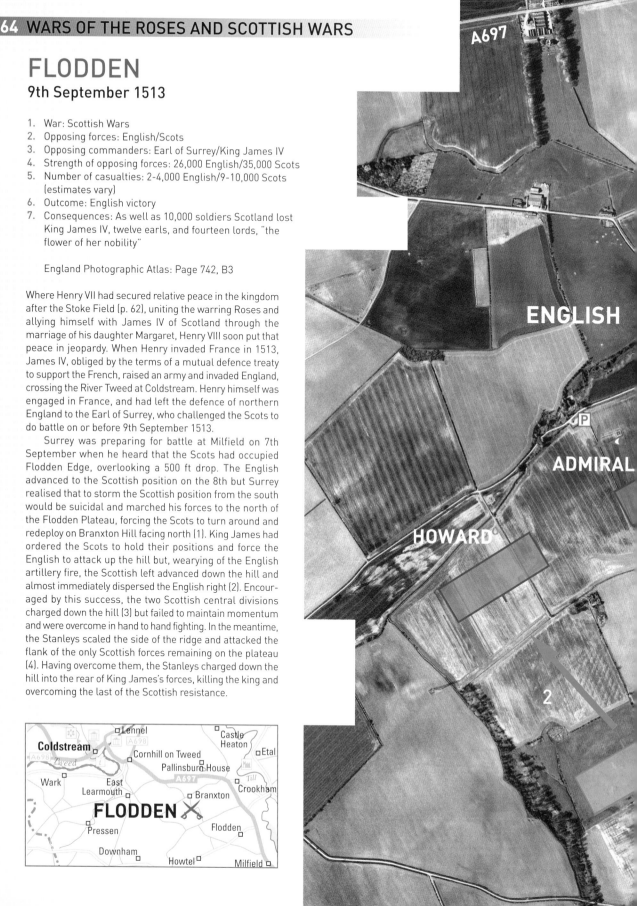

Location: 3 miles south-east from the centre of Coldstream

STANLEY

DACRE

Branxton

SURREY

4

3

3

LENNOX/ ARGYLL

KING JAMES

1

CRAWFORD/ ERROL

BOTHWELL

HOME

SCOTTISH

KEY

Scottish army

English army

viewpoint

P car park

monument

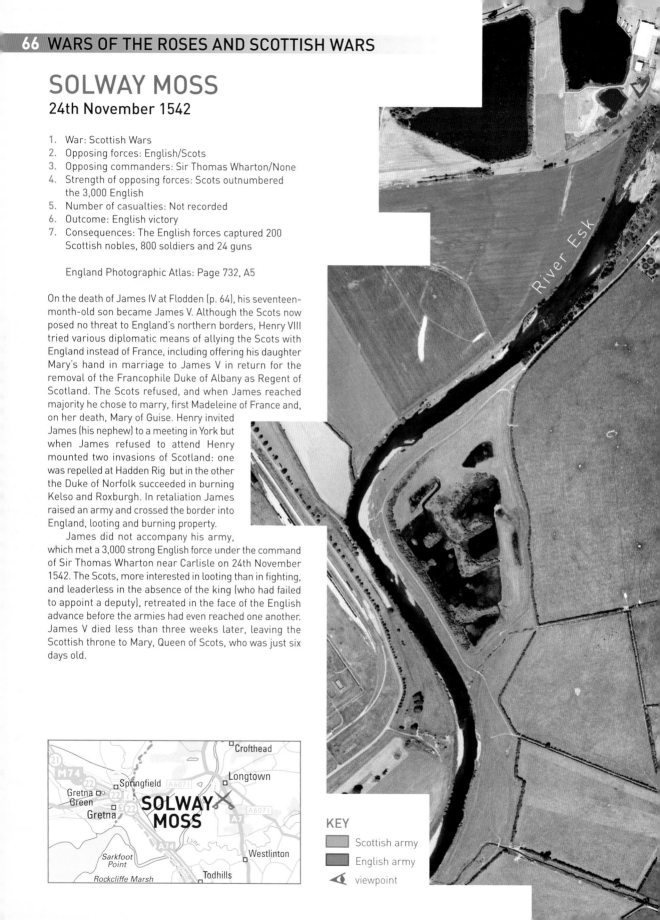

SOLWAY MOSS
24th November 1542

1. War: Scottish Wars
2. Opposing forces: English/Scots
3. Opposing commanders: Sir Thomas Wharton/None
4. Strength of opposing forces: Scots outnumbered the 3,000 English
5. Number of casualties: Not recorded
6. Outcome: English victory
7. Consequences: The English forces captured 200 Scottish nobles, 800 soldiers and 24 guns

England Photographic Atlas: Page 732, A5

On the death of James IV at Flodden (p. 64), his seventeen-month-old son became James V. Although the Scots now posed no threat to England's northern borders, Henry VIII tried various diplomatic means of allying the Scots with England instead of France, including offering his daughter Mary's hand in marriage to James V in return for the removal of the Francophile Duke of Albany as Regent of Scotland. The Scots refused, and when James reached majority he chose to marry, first Madeleine of France and, on her death, Mary of Guise. Henry invited James (his nephew) to a meeting in York but when James refused to attend Henry mounted two invasions of Scotland: one was repelled at Hadden Rig but in the other the Duke of Norfolk succeeded in burning Kelso and Roxburgh. In retaliation James raised an army and crossed the border into England, looting and burning property.

James did not accompany his army, which met a 3,000 strong English force under the command of Sir Thomas Wharton near Carlisle on 24th November 1542. The Scots, more interested in looting than in fighting, and leaderless in the absence of the king (who had failed to appoint a deputy), retreated in the face of the English advance before the armies had even reached one another. James V died less than three weeks later, leaving the Scottish throne to Mary, Queen of Scots, who was just six days old.

River Esk

KEY

Scottish army

English army

◀ viewpoint

Location:
4 miles east
from the
centre of
Gretna

Longtown

SCOTTISH

A7

WHARTON

ENGLISH

ENGLISH CIVIL WARS

NEWBURN FORD
28th August 1640

1. War: Bishops' Wars
2. Opposing forces: English/Scots
3. Opposing commanders: Lord Conway/Alexander Leslie
4. Strength of opposing forces: 5,500 English/20,000 Scots
5. Number of casualties: Not recorded
6. Outcome: Scottish victory
7. Consequences: The financial and political implications of defeat left Charles I with no option but to recall Parliament

England Photographic Atlas: Page 718, B2

Charles I believed in the divine right of the sovereign to rule, and regarded any opposition as treasonous. Faced with MPs opposed to his views, in 1629 Charles dissolved Parliament and ruled autonomously during what became known as the "Eleven Years Tyranny". During this time Charles tried to align the Scottish Presbyterian Church with the Church of England by forcing the Scots to accept a new prayer book and, when the Scots refused, he raised an army to enforce his will.

In 1639, unconvinced of the strength of his army, Charles was forced to accept the terms of the Pacification of Berwick. Characteristically, he reneged on that agreement and took up arms again the following year, prompting the Scottish army to cross the border. The Scots were met at Newburn Ford by a vastly inferior force under Lord Conway, who had been commanded to stop the Scots crossing the Tyne. Leslie's Scottish forces approached the ford from the north (1), bombarding the English line with canon fire from the top of Newburn Church (2). When the Scots began a determined advance across the river (3), the English forces simply turned and quit the field (4).

The so-called battle had been little more than a skirmish but its results were far-reaching. The Scots, in collaboration with Charles' opponents, refused to withdraw from northern England until Charles had recalled Parliament, a demand to which his financial and political situation forced him to accede.

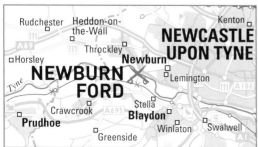

KEY

Scottish army

English army

◀ viewpoint

P car park

Location:
5 miles west
from the
centre of
Newcastle

LESLIE

NEWBURN

CONWAY

1

2

3

EDGEHILL
23rd October 1642

1. War: First Civil War
2. Opposing forces: Parliamentarians/Royalists
3. Opposing commanders: Earl of Essex/King Charles I
4. Strength of opposing forces: 12,000 Parliamentarians/12,000 Royalists
5. Number of casualties: 3,000 in total
6. Outcome: Inconclusive
7. Consequences: The battle petered out with both sides claiming victory, the Parliamentarians retiring to Warwick and the Royalists to Oxford, which became the king's headquarters for the remainder of the First Civil War

England Photographic Atlas: Page 409, G5

Continuing disagreements between king and parliament (see p. 70) led to an attempt by Charles to arrest five MPs on charges of treason. This action met with such opposition that the king was obliged to leave London, and on 22nd August 1642 he raised his standard in Nottingham: the Civil War had begun.

As the Royalist army marched on London, the Parliamentarians moved to block their way, and the two forces met at Edgehill on 23rd October 1642. The Royalists deployed on the ridge of Edgehill, 300 feet above the surrounding plain. The Parliamentarians deployed opposite but there was little reason for them to attack: tactically they did not want to advance up the slope, and politically it would be better for the king to be seen to strike the first blow of a civil war. It was left to Prince Rupert, on the Royalist right, to make the first advance (1), easily overcoming the Parliamentarian left. On the Royalist left Lord Wilmot followed Prince Rupert's lead with similar results (2) leaving the foot soldiers of both armies to fight it out in the centre. The Royalists advanced down the hill (3) but the Parliamentarians held their line, supported by their cavalry which rode out from behind its own foot soldiers to attack the Royalist flank (4). The Royalist cavalry was too exhausted to begin another offensive, and the fighting ended in confusion as night fell.

The battle had been inconclusive, with both sides claiming victory – the Parliamentarians had stood their ground in the face of a Royalist attack, but the Royalists remained free to march on towards London. In the event the king's army made its way instead to Oxford, which became his headquarters for the duration of the war.

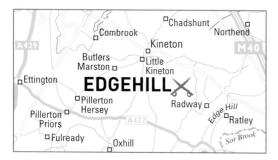

PARLIAMENTARIANS

The Oaks

FIELDI

KEY

	Parliamentarian army
	Parliamentarian cavalry
••••	Parliamentarian skirmishers
	Parliamentarian dragoons
	Royalist army
	Royalist cavalry
	viewpoint
	monument

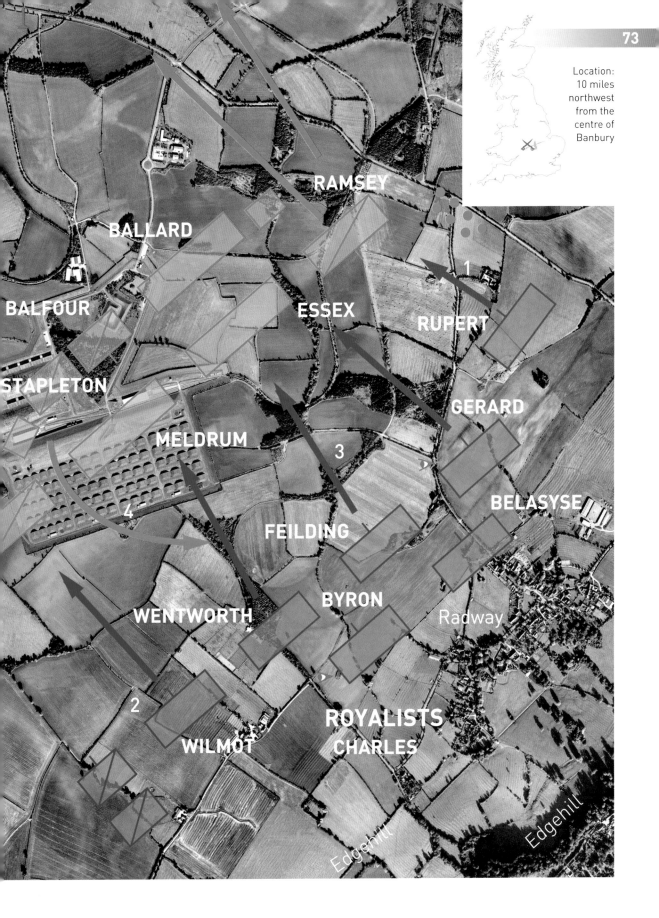

Location: 10 miles northwest from the centre of Banbury

RAMSEY

BALLARD

BALFOUR

ESSEX

RUPERT

1

STAPLETON

GERARD

MELDRUM

3

4

BELASYSE

FEILDING

BYRON

Radway

WENTWORTH

2

WILMOT

ROYALISTS

CHARLES

Edgehill

Edgehill

BRADDOCK DOWN
19th January 1643

1. War: First Civil War
2. Opposing forces: Parliamentarians/Royalists
3. Opposing commanders: Colonel Ruthin/Sir Ralph Hopton
4. Strength of opposing forces: 4,000 Parliamentarians/16,000 Royalists
5. Number of casualties: 1250 Parliamentarians captured
6. Outcome: Royalist victory
7. Consequences: The Parliamentarian Ruthin was prevented from joining forces with the Earl of Stamford

England Photographic Atlas: Page 26, A3

In early 1643 supremacy in the south-west of England had still not been established. Sir Ralph Hopton had established a Royalist army of approximately 16,000 men, but he was threatened by Colonel Ruthin's local Parliamentarians and a force marching south-westwards under the Earl of Stamford. Hopton decided to confront Ruthin's numerically inferior army before Ruthin was able to join forces with Stamford.

The two armies met on 19th January 1643 at Braddock Down close to Liskeard, and drew up on either side of a small valley (1). Neither commander wanted to give up the advantage of the high ground, but eventually Hopton took the initiative, realising that Ruthin's artillery had not been deployed. Sir Bevil Grenville led the Royalist charge across the valley (2), and the Parliamentarians were so shaken by the ferocity of the uphill attack that they turned and fled, abandoning much of their artillery as they did so.

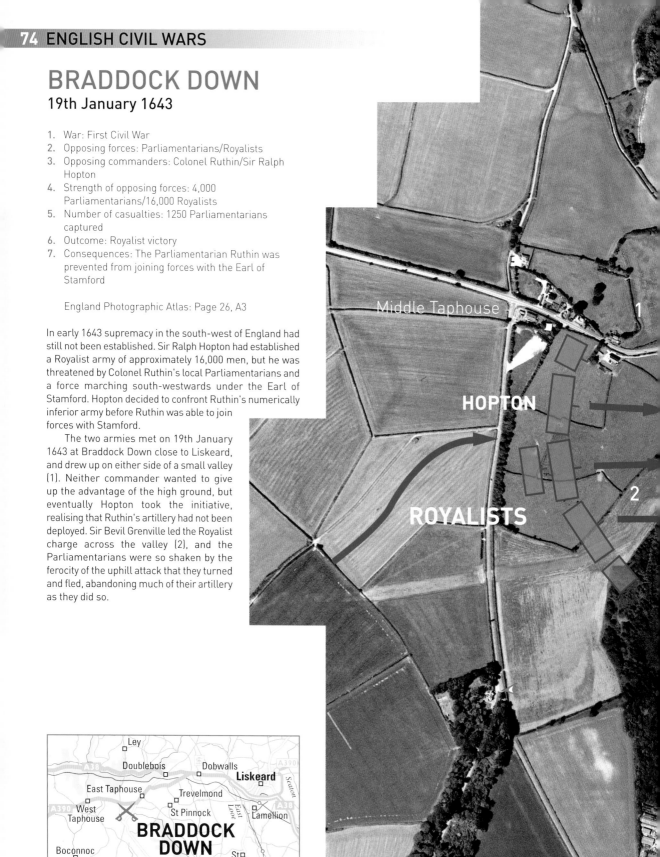

Location:
6 miles east
from the
centre of
Lostwithiel

East Taphouse

A390

RUTHIN

PARLIAMENTARIANS

KEY

Parliamentarian army

Royalist army

viewpoint

HOPTON HEATH
19th March 1643

1. War: First Civil War
2. Opposing forces: Parliamentarians/Royalists
3. Opposing commanders: Sir John Gell and Sir William Brereton/Earl of Northampton
4. Strength of opposing forces: 1,500 Parliamentarians/1,200 Royalists
5. Number of casualties: 300-500
6. Outcome: Royalist victory
7. Consequences: A hollow victory because the Royalist Earl of Northampton was killed in the battle

England Photographic Atlas: Page 494, C4

Sir John Gell and Sir Wiliam Brereton had brought their forces together in order to capture Stafford for the Parliamentarian cause but their plans were disrupted by the arrival of a Royalist army under the command of the Earl of Northampton. The two armies met on 19th March 1643 on Hopton Heath, where the Parliamentarians had deployed (1) on uneven ground that was pockmarked with rabbit holes, making a cavalry charge exceedingly risky while hedges and walls provided defence on the Parliamentarian left.

Northampton's Royalist forces drew up opposite (2), and the Royalist dragoons advanced towards the Parliamentarian musketry covered by fire from "Roaring Meg", a massive Royalist demi-cannon whose destructive powers demoralised the Parliamentarian forces. Northampton followed up his dragoons' advance with a cavalry charge which drove back the Parliamentarian horse but failed to dislodge the foot soldiers, who were said to "perform mighty greate execution". Northampton was killed during this first charge but the Royalist horse regrouped for a second charge. This time the Parliamentarian horse fled the field, but again the foot soldiers did not give way, leaving the outcome of the battle inconclusive as night fell. Technically victory belonged to the Royalists because the Parliamentarians left the field under cover of darkness but it was a victory that gained little tactically, and cost much in the loss of Northampton.

ROYALISTS

Hopton

[Inset map:]
Great Bridgeford · Whitgreave · Yarlet · Gayton · Stowe · Marston · Salt · Weston · Hopton · Hixon · HOPTON HEATH · Ingestre · Great Haywood · Tixall · STAFFORD · Derrington · Castle Bank · Little Haywood

Location:
4 miles north-
east from the
centre of
Stafford

PARLIAMENTARIANS

GELL

1

BRERETON

RAF
Stafford

2

NORTHAMPTON

A518

KEY

Parliamentarian army

Royalist army

viewpoint

STRATTON
16th May 1643

1. War: First Civil War
2. Opposing forces: Parliamentarians/Royalists
3. Opposing commanders: Earl of Stamford & James Chudleigh/Sir Ralph Hopton
4. Strength of opposing forces: 5,500 Parliamentarians/3,000 Royalists
5. Number of casualties: 300 Parliamentarians (1700 prisoners)
6. Outcome: Royalist victory
7. Consequences: Hopton was able to keep his rendezvous with Prince Maurice

England Photographic Atlas: Page 56, C5

As well as the struggle for London, control of local areas was important to the outcome of the Civil War. In the West Country, the Royalists were driven out of Somerset but managed to secure Cornwall at the Battle of Braddock Down. After several skirmishes between the Royalists under Sir Ralph Hopton and the Parliamentarians under James Chudleigh, Chudleigh succeeded in ambushing Hopton at Stourton Down. Among the spoils were letters ordering Hopton to move into Somerset to join forces with Prince Maurice. In order to prevent this, the Parliamentarian Earl of Stamford advanced into Cornwall and deployed an army in an iron age hill fort on the 200-foot rise of Stamford Hill near Stratton (1).

Outnumbered almost 2:1, Hopton decided to use the element of surprise and make a dawn attack. He also took the tactically innovative but risky decision to divide his already small force into four columns in order to attack simultaneously from the north, south and west (2), the east face of the hill being too steep to launch an attack from that direction. After eight hours the Royalists had been unable to make any headway, and Chudleigh ordered the Parliamentarian pikemen to charge. They succeeded in forcing the Royalists down the hill but against all the odds the Royalists rallied and forced Chudleigh's men back up the hill. The Royalist cavalry, held in reserve, now joined the battle and the demoralised Parliamentarians fled their position at the top of the hill.

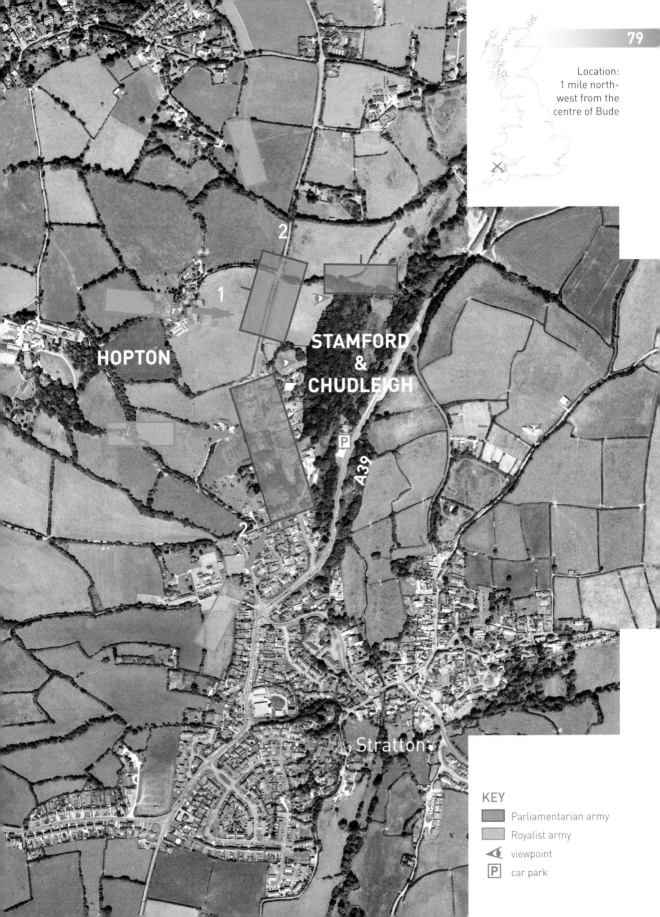

Location:
1 mile north-
west from the
centre of Bude

HOPTON

2

1

STAMFORD
&
CHUDLEIGH

P

A39

2

Stratton

KEY

Parliamentarian army

Royalist army

◄ viewpoint

P car park

ADWALTON MOOR
30th June 1643

1. War: First Civil War
2. Opposing forces: Parliamentarians/Royalists
3. Opposing commanders: Lord Ferdinando Fairfax/Earl of Newcastle
4. Strength of opposing forces: 4,000 Parliamentarians/10,000 Royalists
5. Number of casualties: Not recorded
6. Outcome: Royalist victory
7. Consequences: A decisive battle for the control of Yorkshire: as a result of the Parliamentarian defeat Bradford and Leeds fell to the Royalists, leaving the Earl of Newcastle free to lay siege to Hull

England Photographic Atlas: Page 637, H5

The campaign for control of the north of England was led by the Earl of Newcastle for the Royalists, and by Ferdinando, 2nd Baron Fairfax, and his son Thomas for the Parliamentarians. In mid-1642 much of Yorkshire was held by the Parliamentarians, but a year later the Earl of Newcastle had succeeded in making significant incursions for the Royalists, gaining control of York, Tadcaster, Pontefract Castle, Scarborough and Newark. Parliament took Leeds and Wakefield early in 1643, and the Royalists moved on Bradford June 1643. In order to prevent a siege of the city Fairfax led a small Parliamentarian force out to meet the Royalists, and the unevenly matched armies met on 30th June 1643 at Adwalton Moor, five miles east of Bradford.

Newcastle deployed the Royalist forces on the heights of Adwalton Moor (1) but, rather than engage him there, Fairfax remained among the enclosed fields on the edge of the moor (2), forcing the Royalists to abandon the advantage of the hill in order to attack. The Parliamentarians repelled Newcastle's advance and managed to drive the Royalists back up the hill (3), but Fairfax's success was his own undoing because as the Royalists regained the advantages of the open space, their cavalry and superior numbers could be brought to bear – from the top of the hill the Royalists were able to reverse the Parliamentarian advance and force a crushing retreat (4). As a result of the destruction of the Parliamentarian forces, the Royalists took Leeds and Bradford with no further resistance, and Fairfax was forced to retreat to the Parliamentarian stronghold of Hull.

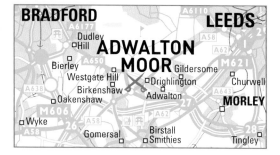

Location:
10 miles
southwest
from the
centre of
Leeds

A 650

3

4

Drighlington

1

NEWCASTLE

KEY

Parliamentarian army

Royalist army

◄ viewpoint

LANSDOWN HILL
5th July 1643

1. War: First Civil War
2. Opposing forces: Parliamentarians/Royalists
3. Opposing commanders: Major-General Sir William Waller/Sir Ralph Hopton
4. Strength of opposing forces: 4,000 Parliamentarians/6,300 Royalists
5. Number of casualties: Not recorded
6. Outcome: Inconclusive
7. Consequences: An inconclusive battle in the campaign for control of the West Country

England Photographic Atlas: Page 102, A6

Sir Ralph Hopton (Royalist) and Sir William Waller (Parliamentarian) were old friends who found themselves fighting for opposing causes, and even wrote to each other before the battle decrying "this war without an enemy". The king had sent extra troops under Prince Maurice to reinforce Hopton's army in the West Country and, following his improbable success at Stratton (p. 78), Hopton was able to join forces with Maurice and attempt to dislodge the Parliamentarians from their stronghold at Bath.

After some minor skirmishing on 4th July 1643, both leaders made for the high ground of Lansdown Hill in order to secure a position. Waller arrived first and deployed the Parliamentarian forces on the crest of the hill (1). Unwilling to attack such a strong position, Hopton withdrew. He returned the following day to find that the Parliamentarians had further fortified their position, and he again withdrew. This time Waller launched a cavalry charge after the retreating Royalists (2) but, instead of causing a rout, this action provoked the Royalist forces into turning and storming the hill (3). Remarkably the uphill assault was not repelled, and after fierce hand-to-hand fighting the Parliamentary forces withdrew to a position further back on the summit of the hill, protected by a stone wall (4). Both armies were now exhausted and, rather than launch further attacks, were content to simply hold their positions. Under the cover of darkness Waller withdrew the Parliamentary forces, leaving their weapons leaning on the wall to give the impression that they were still defending their position. This battle for control of the West Country was inconclusive, but a week later Waller's forces were crushed by the Royalists at Roundway Down (p. 84).

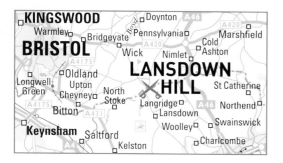

Location:
9 miles east
from the
centre of
Bristol

1

HOPTON

3

2

3

P

1

WALLER

4

KEY

Parliamentarian army

Royalist army

viewpoint

P car park

monument

ROUNDWAY DOWN
13th July 1643

1. War: First Civil War
2. Opposing forces: Parliamentarians/Royalists
3. Opposing commanders: Major-General Sir William Waller/Lord Wilmot, Sir John Byron & Sir Ralph Hopton
4. Strength of opposing forces: 4,500 Parliamentarians/1,800 Royalists
5. Number of casualties: 600 Parliamentarians (800 prisoners)
6. Outcome: Royalist victory
7. Consequences: Sir William Waller's Parliamentary strength in the West Country was all but wiped out

England Photographic Atlas: Page 93, E3

Four days after the inconclusive Battle of Lansdown Hill (p. 82), Hopton's Royalist forces withdrew to Devizes. Hopton had been injured and his forces barricaded the town for a siege. King Charles sent reinforcements under Sir John Wilmot and Sir John Byron, but they found their way blocked by Waller's Parliamentarians, who were deployed in four divisions on Roundway Down (1). Hopton's besieged forces, seeing the Parliamentarians withdraw from the siege, suspected a trap and did not emerge from the town until late in the battle.

As the three brigades of Royalist cavalry approached the Parliamentary forces (2), Sir Arthur Hesilrige, on the Parliamentarian right, made an ill-advised charge (3) which prevented the Parliamentarian musketeers from firing without hitting their own men, and was easily repelled by Wilmot's lighter cavalry (4). Waller then launched his own cavalry at the remaining Royalist divisions (5) with similar results (6). The Royalists pursued Waller's forces as far as Oliver's Castle, where the ground falls away in a 300-foot drop. Riding too fast to rein in, many of the fleeing Parliamentarians were killed falling into the "Bloody Ditch" (7).

The Parliamentarian infantry, who had thus far been spectators to the cavalry charges, now found themselves surprised by the arrival of Hopton's Royalist infantry to their rear (8), who had been convinced by the sounds of battle that this was not a Parliamentarian ruse and that reinforcements had indeed arrived. The sudden arrival of so many fresh troops put the Parliamentarians to flight, and the Royalists had gained control of the West Country.

Oliver's Castle
prehistoric camp

KEY

Parliamentarian army

Royalist army

viewpoint

P car park

CRAWFORD

BYRON

2

WILMOT

6

5

4

WALLER

1

3

HESILRIGE

Bishops
Cannings

NEWBURY
20th September 1643

1. War: First Civil War
2. Opposing forces: Parliamentarians/Royalists
3. Opposing commanders: Earl of Essex/King Charles I
4. Strength of opposing forces: 14,000 Parliamentarians/14,000 Royalists
5. Number of casualties: 3,500 in total
6. Outcome: Parliamentarian victory
7. Consequences: The King had failed in his attempt to prevent Essex returning to London

England Photographic Atlas: Page 185, G2

In August 1643 King Charles and his army laid siege to Gloucester, but withdrew early in September to avoid a confrontation with a force of 14,000 men under the Earl of Essex arriving to relieve the city. Although Gloucester was once again under Parliamentary control, the king had succeeded in drawing Essex away from London, and now moved to prevent Essex's return. The Royalist army arrived at Newbury a few hours ahead of Essex on 19th September 1643 and set up defensive positions to the west of the town (1), effectively blocking Essex's path to London and forcing him to do battle.

Having arrived at Newbury first, the King lost the initiative by failing to secure Round Hill, and was surprised at dawn by artillery fire from the Parliamentarians who had deployed under cover of darkness (2) and secured the strategic position of the hill for themselves. Sir John Byron, in the Royalist centre, advanced (3) and briefly gained the Round Hill before being driven back, and fighting elsewhere in the field followed a similar pattern with the Royalists gaining ground and then losing it, not helped by the fact that a large number of the Royalist foot soldiers found cover and refused to take any further part in the battle. At nightfall neither side had gained any significant advantage and the fighting ended in stalemate. The Earl of Essex probably expected the battle to continue the following day but found that the king, who was running short of ammunition, had withdrawn during the night to Oxford, giving Essex a surprise victory and leaving the Parliamentarians free to complete their return to London.

SKIPTON

A34

ESS

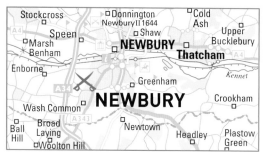

KEY

	Parliamentarian army
	Parliamentarian cavalry
	Royalist army
	Royalist cavalry
◄	viewpoint
P	car park
⊥	monument

Location:
2 miles south-
west from the
centre of
Newbury

VASAVOUR

BYRON

CHARLES

Round Hill

RUPERT

NANTWICH
25th January 1644

1. War: First Civil War
2. Opposing forces: Parliamentarians/Royalists
3. Opposing commanders: Sir Thomas Fairfax/Lord John Byron
4. Strength of opposing forces: 5,000 Parliamentarians/5,000 Royalists
5. Number of casualties: 200 Royalists (1,500 prisoners)
6. Outcome: Parliamentarian victory
7. Consequences: Victory for the Parliamentarians broke the Royalist domination of Cheshire

England Photographic Atlas: Page 521, F5

Towards the end of 1643 King Charles arranged for five regiments of Irish foot soldiers to bolster Royalist forces in the north-west where, under Lord John Byron, they succeeded in taking control of most of Cheshire. Byron laid siege to Nantwich in December, but on 25th January 1644 he was confronted by a Parliamentarian force commanded by Sir Thomas Fairfax, who intended to break the siege.

Learning of Fairfax's approach, Byron deployed his Royalist troops on high ground near Acton (1) but his position was so strong that Fairfax refused to do battle, marching instead across country in front of the Royalist lines (2). Byron's left wing advanced on the tail of Fairfax's column, forcing them to turn and fight (3), while his right wing engaged the head of the Parliamentarian column (4). The Parliamentarian column now turned to face the Royalist flank attack (5), overwhelming the Royalist centre in the difficult terrain. The Royalists were driven towards Acton, where Parliamentary reinforcements were waiting and where 1,500 Royalists surrendered, leaving the Parliamentarians in control of Cheshire.

KEY

	Parliamentarian army
	Royalist army
◀	viewpoint
P	car park

Location: 1 miles north-west from the centre of Nantwich

A51

FAIRFAX

2

5

YRON

1

4

P

NANTWICH

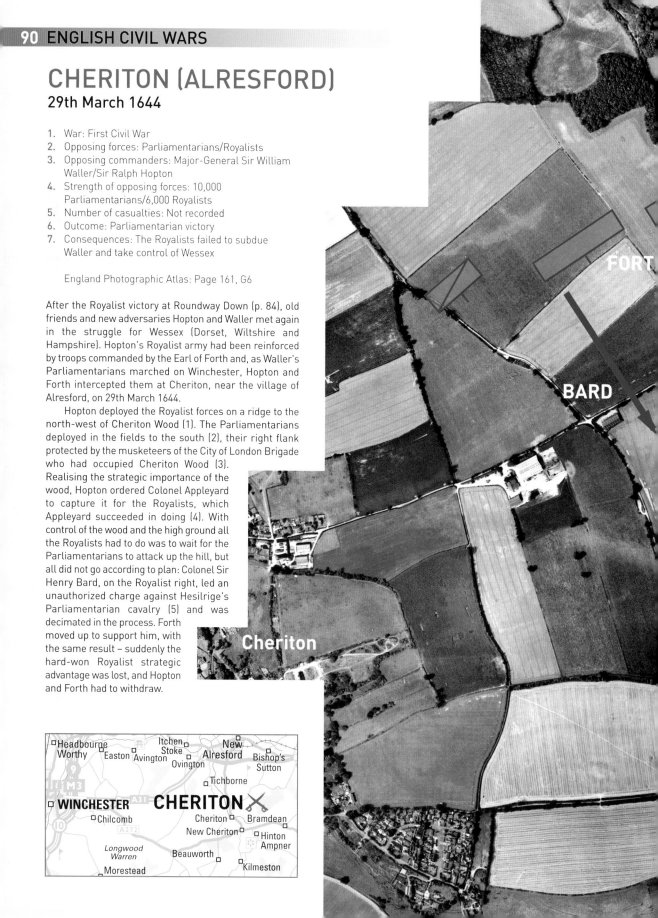

CHERITON (ALRESFORD)
29th March 1644

1. War: First Civil War
2. Opposing forces: Parliamentarians/Royalists
3. Opposing commanders: Major-General Sir William Waller/Sir Ralph Hopton
4. Strength of opposing forces: 10,000 Parliamentarians/6,000 Royalists
5. Number of casualties: Not recorded
6. Outcome: Parliamentarian victory
7. Consequences: The Royalists failed to subdue Waller and take control of Wessex

England Photographic Atlas: Page 161, G6

After the Royalist victory at Roundway Down (p. 84), old friends and new adversaries Hopton and Waller met again in the struggle for Wessex (Dorset, Wiltshire and Hampshire). Hopton's Royalist army had been reinforced by troops commanded by the Earl of Forth and, as Waller's Parliamentarians marched on Winchester, Hopton and Forth intercepted them at Cheriton, near the village of Alresford, on 29th March 1644.

Hopton deployed the Royalist forces on a ridge to the north-west of Cheriton Wood (1). The Parliamentarians deployed in the fields to the south (2), their right flank protected by the musketeers of the City of London Brigade who had occupied Cheriton Wood (3). Realising the strategic importance of the wood, Hopton ordered Colonel Appleyard to capture it for the Royalists, which Appleyard succeeded in doing (4). With control of the wood and the high ground all the Royalists had to do was to wait for the Parliamentarians to attack up the hill, but all did not go according to plan: Colonel Sir Henry Bard, on the Royalist right, led an unauthorized charge against Hesilrige's Parliamentarian cavalry (5) and was decimated in the process. Forth moved up to support him, with the same result – suddenly the hard-won Royalist strategic advantage was lost, and Hopton and Forth had to withdraw.

FORT

BARD

Cheriton

Headbourne Worthy · Itchen Stoke · New Alresford · Bishop's Sutton · Easton · Avington · Ovington · Tichborne · WINCHESTER · CHERITON · Chilcomb · Cheriton · Bramdean · New Cheriton · Hinton Ampner · Longwood Warren · Beauworth · Kilmeston · Morestead

Location:
10 miles west
from the
centre of
Winchester

APPLEYARD

ROYALISTS

1

4

Cheriton Wood

3

musketeers

BALFOUR

2

5

WALLER

PARLIAMENTARIANS

HESILRIGE

PTON

KEY

Parliamentarian army
Parliamentarian cavalry
Royalist army
Royalist cavalry
viewpoint

CROPREDY BRIDGE
29th June 1644

1. War: First Civil War
2. Opposing forces: Parliamentarians/Royalists
3. Opposing commanders: Major-General Sir William Waller/King Charles I
4. Strength of opposing forces: 8,500 Parliamentarians/9,000 Royalists
5. Number of casualties: 700 Parliamentarians (including deserters)
6. Outcome: Inconclusive
7. Consequences: Waller failed to destroy the Royalist army

England Photographic Atlas: Page 410, C6

After his success at Cheriton (p. 90), Waller moved further east and began operations against the main Royalist army close to its headquarters at Oxford. In June 1644 part of the Parliamentary force, under the Earl of Essex, was sent to relieve the siege of Lyme and the King took the opportunity to march on Waller's reduced numbers. Deciding against a direct attack on Waller's base at Hanwell Castle, the Royalist army moved northward on the eastern side of the River Cherwell. Waller shadowed this march on the western side of the river, with both armies in view of each other.

Waller saw that the Royalist forces had become strung out, with a large gap appearing between the van and the rearguard. Between the two halves of the king's forces lay Cropredy Bridge, and behind the rearguard was a ford, so Waller decided to attack the Royalist rearguard with a pincer movement across the river. Dividing his own forces, Waller took 1,000 men across the river at Slat Mill Ford (1), to the south of the Royalist rearguard, sending Lieutenant-General John Middleton to cross at Cropredy Bridge (2) to the north. However, Waller had not counted on the skill of the Earl of Northampton, who forced the Parliamentarians back across the ford (3), or the resistance of the Earl of Cleveland, who held Middleton's forces until the Royalist vanguard, realising what was happening behind them, turned in support and forced Middleton back across the bridge.

The Parliamentarian rearguard prevented the Royalists from crossing the bridge in pursuit and the battle ended inconclusively. Learning of 4,500 Parliamentarians marching to reinforce Waller, the Royalist forces withdrew the following day.

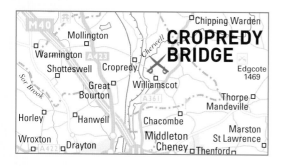

Location:
3 miles north
from the
centre of
Oxford

CHARLES

ROYALISTS

CLEVELAND

4

ASTLEY

3

NORTHAMPTON

WALLER

KEY

Parliamentarian army

Parliamentarian cavalry

Royalist army

Royalist cavalry

viewpoint

P car park

MARSTON MOOR
2nd July 1644

1. War: First Civil War
2. Opposing forces: Royalists/Scots & Parliamentarians
3. Opposing commanders: Prince Rupert & Earl of Newcastle/Earl of Manchester, Earl of Leven & Lord Fairfax
4. Strength of opposing forces: 18,000 Royalists/27,000 Scots & Parliamentarians
5. Number of casualties: 6,000 in total
6. Outcome: Parliamentarian victory
7. Consequences: The Royalists lost control of the north of England and the Earl of Newcastle fled to the continent

England Photographic Atlas: Page 663, H4

In 1633 the Parliamentarians signed the Solemn League and Covenant with the Scots, forcing the Royalists to fight the war on two fronts. The Royalist Earl of Newcastle withstood the Scots until April when the Scottish forces joined the northern Parliamentarians and laid siege to York. In June 1644 Prince Rupert set out to relieve York and linked up with the Earl of Newcastle, who was defending the besieged city. On 2nd July the Royalists confronted the allied forces of the Scots and the Parliamentarians at Marston Moor.

Prince Rupert deployed the Royalist army on flat ground protected by a ditch and bank (1). The allied forces began to withdraw, preferring to intercept the Royalists on their return south – Prince Rupert decided to attack the weakened rearguard but was unable to act quickly enough. While he waited for Newcastle's troops, who had not yet left York, the main body of the allied force, realising the danger, had time to return to the field and deploy along the ridge of Marston Hill. In the late afternoon Cromwell, on the Parliamentarian left, charged and routed Lord Byron's cavalry on the Royalist right (2). At the other end of the line the reverse occurred, with Lord Goring's Royalists charging and routing the Parliamentarian cavalry (3). In the centre the Royalist foot soldiers were making progress against the superior numbers of the Parliamentarians (4), but it was the discipline of Cromwell's cavalry that won the day: instead of pursuing Byron's cavalry they regrouped and now charged in support of their foot soldiers, turning the tide of the battle against the Royalists. Newcastle's Royalist Whitecoats famously fought to the last but the battle was lost, and with it Royalist control of the north of England.

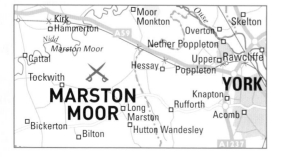

BYRON

Tockwith

CROMWELL

LESLIE

MANCHESTER

KEY

Parliamentarian army
Parliamentarian cavalry
Royalist army
Royalist cavalry
Royalist skirmishers
viewpoint
car park
monument

Location:
8 miles west
from the
centre of York

RUPERT

1

NEWCASTLE (WHITE COATS)

GORING

4

CRAWFORD

BAILLIE

LUMSDEN

3

T. FAIRFAX

SCOTTISH
CAVALRY

Long
Marston

F. FAIRFAX

NASEBY
14th June 1645

1. War: First Civil War
2. Opposing forces: Parliamentarians/Royalists
3. Opposing commanders: Sir Thomas Fairfax/King Charles I
4. Strength of opposing forces: 13,500 Parliamentarians/9,000 Royalists
5. Number of casualties: 200 Parliamentarians/1,000 Royalists
6. Outcome: Parliamentarian victory
7. Consequences: The battle that effectively decided the war in Parliament's favour. Charles's correspondence was captured and published by Parliament as proof of his duplicity

England Photographic Atlas: Page 462, D5

Within a year of their success at Marston Moor (p. 94) the Parliamentarians had amalgamated the three armies of William Waller and the Earls of Essex and Manchester into the New Model Army under the command of Sir Thomas Fairfax. Fairfax laid siege to the Royalist headquarters of Oxford and, rather than challenge him directly, the Royalists laid siege to Leicester in order to lure Fairfax away from Oxford. In this they were overly successful, provoking a pursuit by Fairfax that forced the Royalists to turn and do battle at Naseby on 14th June 1645.

After some initial manoeuvring the two armies deployed opposite each other on the undulating ground now known as Broadmoor, the Royalists to the north (1) and the Parliamentarians to the south, just back from the crest of a ridge that hid the full extent of their forces from the Royalists (2). The battle followed a similar pattern to Marston Moor, with Prince Rupert's cavalry charge on the Royalist right succeeding in routing the greater part of the Parliamentarian left (3) and Cromwell having reciprocal success on the Parliamentarian right (4). Again as at Marston Moor, Rupert's cavalry left the field in pursuit of the fleeing enemy, while Cromwell's regrouped to make a flanking attack on the Royalist infantry, which until that point had been driving the Parliamentarians back. This action won the battle for the Parliamentarians who went on to capture the Royalist baggage train including King Charles's private correspondence, which was published by Parliament and played a key role in the king's eventual downfall.

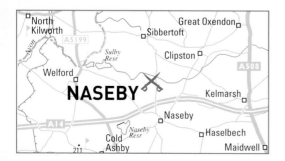

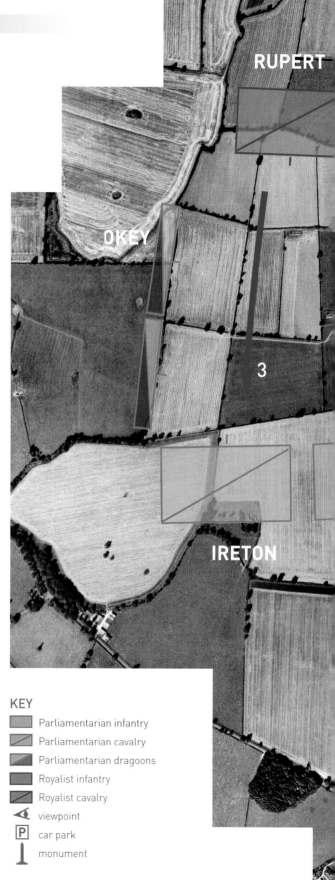

KEY

Parliamentarian infantry
Parliamentarian cavalry
Parliamentarian dragoons
Royalist infantry
Royalist cavalry
◀ viewpoint
P car park
⌐ monument

Location:
12 miles west
from the
centre of
Kettering

ASTLEY

LANGDALE

1

ROYALISTS

P

2

4

FAIRFAX

CROMWELL

PARLIAMENTARIANS

A14

LANGPORT
10th July 1645

1. War: First Civil War
2. Opposing forces: Parliamentarians/Royalists
3. Opposing commanders: Sir Thomas Fairfax/General George Goring
4. Strength of opposing forces: 10,000 Parliamentarians/7,000 Royalists
5. Number of casualties: Not recorded
6. Outcome: Parliamentarian victory
7. Consequences: Royalist defeat led eventually to the fall of Bridgwater, leaving the remaining Royalist West Country strongholds in a vulnerable position

England Photographic Atlas: Page 76, C6

Sir Thomas Fairfax continued his decimation of the Royalist cause with a campaign to win the West Country, having secured the north of England for the Parliamentarians at Marston Moor the previous year and the Midlands with victory at Naseby less than a month before the Battle of Langport. The Royalist General George Goring was preparing to meet Fairfax near Langport but as Fairfax approached Goring decided instead to withdraw to Bridgwater. He sent most of his cannon and supplies ahead on 9th June but before he could withdraw his forces, Fairfax attacked. The Battle took place on 10th July 1645, the day after Goring had dispatched his heavy weaponry.

The Royalists were outnumbered and were without most of their cannon but nonetheless felt secure in their position fronted by marshy ground that was only passable by a narrow ford (1). Goring posted two Royalist regiments to defend the ford, supported by his last two cannon, but these were easily overcome by Fairfax's artillery. Fairfax then launched an audacious Parliamentarian cavalry charge across the ford, which could only be crossed four abreast (2). In failing to repulse this charge Goring lost the battle: the initial Parliamentarian advance was backed up by more cavalry and then the Parliamentarian foot soldiers, forcing the Royalists into a retreat. Goring was unable to secure Bridgwater, and the Royalist cause in the West Country was all but lost.

KEY

Parliamentarian army

Parliamentarian cavalry

Royalist army

viewpoint

Location:
16 miles east
from the
centre of
Taunton

2

1

FAIRFAX

Pibsbury

ROWTON HEATH
24th September 1645

1. War: First Civil War
2. Opposing forces: Parliamentarians/Royalists
3. Opposing commanders: General Sydenham Poyntz/Sir Marmaduke Langdale
4. Strength of opposing forces: Not recorded
5. Number of casualties: Not recorded
6. Outcome: Parliamentarian victory
7. Consequences: A relatively minor battle but one that saw the king's last hopes disappear

England Photographic Atlas: Page 519, F1

After defeat at Naseby (p. 96), Charles I's only hopes were to gain further reinforcements from Ireland or to link up with the hitherto successful Montrose. Charles marched north, and on 23rd September 1645 successfully relieved the Royalist garrison in the besieged city of Chester. Historians differ on whether raising the siege should be counted a strategic success or a distraction from the king's purpose: it did secure a base for links with Ireland and Montrose but the king might have been better joining Montrose in Scotland than waiting for him in Chester. However, unbeknownst to Charles, he would have been unable to join Montrose in either case because the latter's forces had been destroyed at Philiphaugh on 13th September.

On 24th September, the day after the relief of Chester, the Royalist cavalry under Sir Marmaduke Langdale set out to destroy the Parliamentarian besiegers of the city, but the Royalists were surprised at Rowton Heath by Parliamentarian cavalry arriving in support of the besiegers under the command of General Sydenham Poyntz (1). Both cavalry divisions sent for reinforcements. Parliamentarian musketeers from the besieging force arrived first, covering Poyntz's advance (2), and by the time Royalist reinforcements arrived from Chester it was too late. King Charles watched from the city walls as his cavalry, and with it the last of his hopes, was destroyed.

Scene of later action

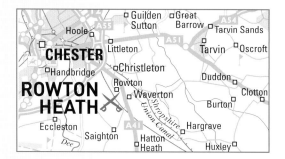

KEY

▨ Parliamentarian infantry

▨ Parliamentarian cavalry

▨ Royalist forces

◄ viewpoint

Location:
1 mile south-
east from the
centre of
Chester

Rowton

A41

River
Dee

Waverton

LANGDALE

2

POYNTZ

1

STOW-ON-THE-WOLD
21st March 1646

1. War: First Civil War
2. Opposing forces: Parliamentarians/Royalists
3. Opposing commanders: Sir William Brereton/Sir Jacob Astley
4. Strength of opposing forces: 3,000 Royalists
5. Number of casualties: Not recorded
6. Outcome: Parliamentarian victory
7. Consequences: The war had already been all but won by the Parliamentarians, this late skirmish doing nothing to change that

England Photographic Atlas: Page 631, E4

After the defeat of Charles I at Rowton Heath and the Marquis of Montrose at Philiphaugh, there was little hope left for the Royalist cause. The king charged Sir Jacob Astley with the job of raising an army, but it was a desperate measure: Astley's force would be able to do little more than prolong the inevitable. Astley managed to raise 3,000 men and marched with them to join the king at Oxford but he was intercepted by Sir William Brereton at Stow-on-the-Wold, where battle took place on 21st March 1646.

Both armies were deployed opposite each other by dawn (1), with Astley having the advantage of the high ground. However, this did not deter the Parliamentarians, who advanced up the slope towards Astley's line (2). The Royalists managed to force the Parliamentarian left into a retreat but on their own left the ferocity of Brereton's cavalry charge forced the Royalist horse from the field, followed by the infantry (3), many of whom were trapped and killed in the market square of Stow-on-the-Wold, just over a mile to the south. If there was little hope for the Royalists before this battle, now there was none at all.

KEY

▨ Parliamentarian army

▨ Royalist army

◀ viewpoint

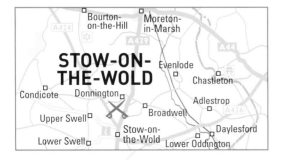

Location:
1.5 miles
north from the
centre of
Stow-on-
the-Wold

2

1

ASTLEY

Donnington

A429

retreat to
Stow-on-the-Wold

WORCESTER
3rd September 1651

1. War: Third Civil War
2. Opposing forces: Parliamentarians/Royalists
3. Opposing commanders: Oliver Cromwell/King Charles II & David Leslie
4. Strength of opposing forces: 28,000 Parliamentarians/16,000 Royalists
5. Number of casualties: Not recorded
6. Outcome: Parliamentarian victory
7. Consequences: Charles II failed in his bid to regain the throne by force, and escaped to France

England Photographic Atlas: Page 404, B3

Although the Civil Wars seemed over with the execution of Charles, the Scots were prepared to accept Charles's son as King Charles II if he agreed to implement the terms of the Solemn League and Covenant, and he was duly proclaimed King in July 1650. Expecting an attack from the north, Cromwell launched a pre-emptive strike, defeating David Leslie's Royalist army at Dunbar in the first battle of the Third Civil War. After several months of skirmishing, the Royalist forces turned southwards to march on London and in August 1651 crossed the border with Cromwell in pursuit.

Heavily outnumbered, Charles took refuge at Worcester, where he destroyed two bridges across the Severn in an attempt to force Cromwell to attack the fortified eastern side of the city. In response Cromwell used barges to create pontoon bridges, allowing Lieutenant-General Charles Fleetwood to launch an attack from the south-west (1), while Cromwell attacked from the east (2). Fleetwood met with fierce resistance from the Royalists and Cromwell led three brigades to his assistance (3), weakening his right flank. Seeing this from the cathedral tower, Charles II led a force out of the eastern gate of the city (4) and was able to hold the Parliamentarians until the return of Cromwell from the left flank turned the battle in their favour, as the Royalists were driven back into the city where many of them were killed in hand to hand fighting.

Charles made his famous escape to France, the Royalist forces surrendered, and the Civil Wars were at an end. However, the Parliamentarian victory was ultimately to no avail, because in-fighting, mistrust and disillusionment with the Parliamentary government led to Charles's restoration to the throne less than ten years later on 29th May 1660.

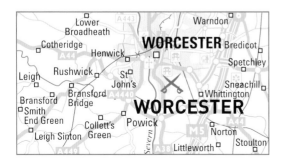

LESLIE

WORCESTER

ROYALISTS

CHARLES

4

CHESHIRE & ESSEX
MILITIA

PARLIAMENTARIANS

2

CROMWELL

3

M5

KEY
Parliamentarian infantry
Parliamentarian cavalry
Royalist infantry
Royalist cavalry
◀ viewpoint
P car park

ANGLO-DUTCH WARS TO THE NAPOLEONIC WARS

MEDWAY INVASION
10th–14th June 1667

1. War: Second Anglo-Dutch War
2. Opposing forces: Dutch navy/English navy
3. Opposing commanders: Admiral de Ruyter/General-at-Sea George Monck
4. Strength of opposing forces: Not recorded
5. Number of casualties: 5 British ships lost, two captured and two scuppered to block the river
6. Outcome: Dutch victory
7. Consequences: De Ruyter blockaded London and a peace treaty was signed at Breda on 31st July

England Photographic Atlas: Page 198/9 & 248/9

There were three Anglo-Dutch Wars, in 1652–54, 1665–67 and 1672–74. The first was precipitated by the Commonwealth Rump Parliament, which was successful in securing commercial supremacy over the Dutch, and the second, after the Restoration, was initiated by the Duke of York (later James II) in an attempt to extend the commercial success of the first war into total victory over the Dutch navy. He defeated the Dutch in the Battle of Lowestoft (1665) and the two navies won a battle each in 1666. However, a combination of heavy losses in battle, the Plague, and the Great Fire of London disabled the English fleet, which in June 1667 was laid up near Chatham on the River Medway, where it was attacked by the Dutch.

The Medway was protected by shore defences and a chain stretched across the river close to Sheerness to form a boom, but the Dutch navy succeeded in breaking through the boom on 10th June and attacking the unmanned English fleet at anchor, sinking five ships and capturing two others including the Royal Charles, part of which is still in the National Museum in Amsterdam. Monck ordered two ships to be sunk further upstream to prevent the Dutch encroaching further. After a month-long blockade of London, the Treaty of Breda allowed the Dutch to bring imports to England, thus weakening the commercial supremacy won in the first war, but the treaty did eventually result in English possession of the New Netherlands, which saw New Amsterdam renamed New York.

The third war was intended to destroy the Dutch Republic but failed in its objectives and was such an unpopular campaign that Parliament withdrew funding for the war and Charles II was forced to make peace.

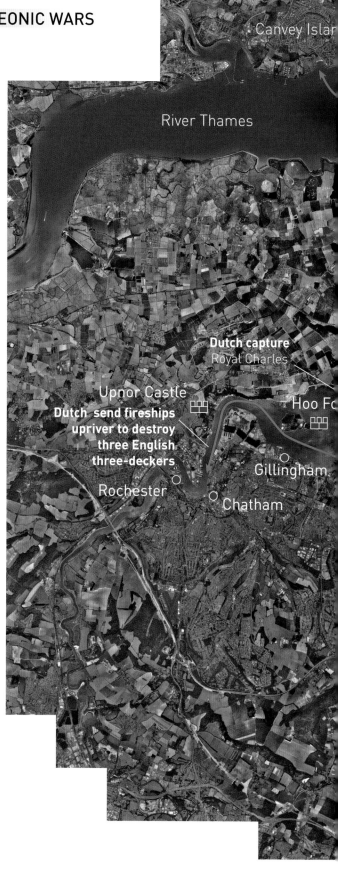

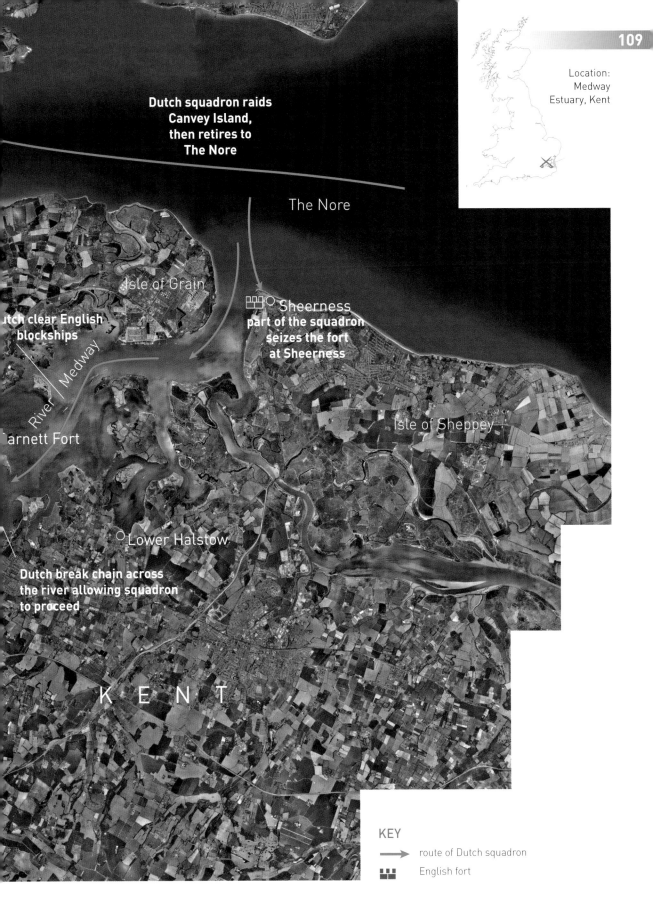

Location:
Medway
Estuary, Kent

Dutch squadron raids
Canvey Island,
then retires to
The Nore

The Nore

Isle of Grain

Dutch clear English
blockships

Sheerness
part of the squadron
seizes the fort
at Sheerness

River Medway

arnett Fort

Isle of Sheppey

○Lower Halstow

Dutch break chain across
the river allowing squadron
to proceed

K E N T

KEY

→ route of Dutch squadron

English fort

SEDGEMOOR
Night of 5th–6th July 1685

1. War: Monmouth Rebellion
2. Opposing forces: Rebels/Royalists
3. Opposing commanders: Duke of Monmouth/Earl of Feversham
4. Strength of opposing forces: 3-4,000 Rebels/2,500 Royalists
5. Number of casualties: 1,000 Rebels/200 Royalists
6. Outcome: Royalist victory
7. Consequences: Monmouth's attempt to gain the throne had failed, and he was beheaded just over a week later on 15th July

England Photographic Atlas: Page 76, A4

England remained relatively peaceful during the reign of Charles II but within a year of his death war broke out in the first of a series of uprisings that were destined to recur sporadically for the next 61 years until the Jacobite cause was finally crushed at Culloden (p. 116). Charles had failed to produce a legal heir and on his death the crown passed to his brother James, who was deeply unpopular because of his Roman Catholicism. The Duke of Monmouth, Charles's oldest illegitimate child, became the champion of the Protestants, and landed from exile in Holland at Lyme Regis on 11th June 1685 to claim the throne.

James II sent an army under the Earl of Feversham to quash the rebel forces and on 5th July 1685, having discovered that the rebels were at Bridgwater, the Royalists set up camp three miles away on Sedgemoor (1), protected by a waterlogged ditch known as the Bussex Rhyne. Monmouth, fearing that his untrained rebel forces would be no match for the Royalist soldiers in a pitched battle, decided to risk a night attack and crossed Sedgemoor towards the Royalist line (2). Discovered less than a mile from the camp by a Royalist sentry, the rebels lost the element of surprise. Monmouth sent Lord Grey's cavalry to cross the Bussex Rhyne and attack the Royalist flank (3) but in the darkness and confusion Grey missed the bridge and collided with a Royalist patrol, resulting in the rebel cavalry fleeing the field (4). The advancing rebel infantry lost its momentum before reaching the Rhine, and instead fired wildly into the night. At dawn Feversham dispatched the Royalist cavalry over river crossings to the east and west of his line to make flanking attacks on the rebel line, which broke and fled the field. The Monmouth Rebellion had been crushed.

KEY

Rebel army

Royal army

◀ viewpoint

Location:
3 miles east
from the
centre of
Bridgwater

2

Moor Drove
Rhyne

GREY

4

3

MONMOUTH

Bussex
Rhyne

FAVERSHAM

1

Westonzoyland

KILLIEKRANKIE
27th July 1689

1. War: Jacobite Rebellion
2. Opposing forces: Jacobites/Scottish government army
3. Opposing commanders: Viscount Dundee/General Hugh Mackay
4. Strength of opposing forces: 2,500 Jacobites/5,000 Government soldiers
5. Number of casualties: 1,200 Jacobites/1,250 Government soldiers
6. Outcome: Jacobite victory
7. Consequences: Although the Jacobites were victorious their leader, Viscount Dundee, was shot and killed

James II's army succeeded in crushing the Monmouth Rebellion at Sedgemoor (p. 110) but the birth of a male heir, securing a Catholic succession, was too much for the English lords. They offered the crown to Prince William of Orange and his wife Mary (James's daughter by his first, Protestant, marriage), and William duly seized the crown as William III in 1688. William and Mary were handed the Scottish crown the following year but Viscount Dundee, commander of James II's forces in Scotland, raised the King's standard in April 1689 to begin the first Jacobite Rebellion. The Scottish government raised an army to crush Dundee's rebels, and on 27th July 1689 the two forces met at Killiecrankie Pass.

As the government army made its way through the pass Mackay saw the Jacobites waiting for him, and manoeuvred his forces to the right in order to gain the high ground. However, when Mackay reached the crest of the ridge he found the Jacobites already occupying a higher ridge beyond. Mackay deployed his forces in "half battalions" (1), increasing the width of the line and therefore his firepower, but reducing his strength in depth, vital in the face of a charge. Dundee responded by widening the gaps between his regiments rather than by thinning them (2), maintaining their depth, and after a two hour wait the Jacobites streamed down the hill into the government ranks (3). A first volley of musket fire felled some 600 Jacobites but the momentum of the charge carried the remainder into the government lines before the musketeers could reload, where the Jacobites had the best of the hand-to-hand fighting. A desperate cavalry charge by Mackay was repelled by Dundee's cavalry (4), but Dundee was shot and killed. Although the battle was won, the first Jacobite Rebellion, now leaderless, petered out with defeats at the Battles of Dunkeld (1689) and Cromdale (1690).

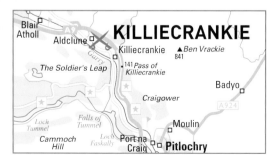

GOVERNMENT ARMY

KEY

▨	Jacobite infantry
▨	Jacobite cavalry
▨	Government infantry
▨	Government cavalry
◀	viewpoint
Ⓟ	car park

Location:
3 miles north
from the
centre of
Pitlochry

2

JACOBITES

2

DUNDEE

A9

3

4

1

MACKAY

River
Garry

Killiecrankie

P

SHERIFFMUIR
13th November 1715

1. War: Jacobite Rebellion
2. Opposing forces: Hanoverians/Jacobites
3. Opposing commanders: Duke of Argyll/Earl of Mar
4. Strength of opposing forces: 3,500 Hanoverians/7,000 Jacobites
5. Number of casualties: 700 Hanoverians/250 Jacobites
6. Outcome: Inconclusive
7. Consequences: Although not defeated, the Earl of Mar retreated to Aberdeen and eventually to France, and the 1715 Jacobite Rebellion petered out as had the first twenty-five years earlier

None of Queen Anne's children survived to adulthood, so parliament passed the Act of Settlement in 1701 in order to prevent a Jacobite restoration, settling the succession on James I's grand-daughter the Electress of Hanover. The Electress died two months before Queen Anne, so it was James I's great-grandson, the Elector of Hanover, who succeeded Queen Anne as George I in 1714. The following year the Earl of Mar took it upon himself to raise the Jacobite "Restoration Standard", though he was probably acting out of self-interest and without the authority of James Stuart, the Pretender to the throne. He marched southwards to join forces with the Jacobites in England but found his way blocked at Dunblane by the Hanoverian government army under the Duke of Argyll, and on 13th November 1715 the two armies met at Sheriffmuir.

The opposing forces were misaligned, each overlapping the other on the right, and as the Jacobites advanced towards the Hanoverians they attempted to realign themselves, the left wing falling into disarray in the process. As a result the Jacobite left was driven back by the Hanoverian right (1) but at the other end of the line the Jacobite advance had succeeded — the Hanoverians were driven back (2) and the battle swung on its axis. The remains of both forces regrouped but, after an abortive advance by the Jacobites, there was no further fighting. Both leaders withdrew at dusk, each claiming victory, although the moral victory lay with the Hanoverians who had survived the onslaught of a force more than twice its size. With its troops demoralized, the Jacobite Rebellion petered out, just as the first uprising had done a quarter of a century earlier.

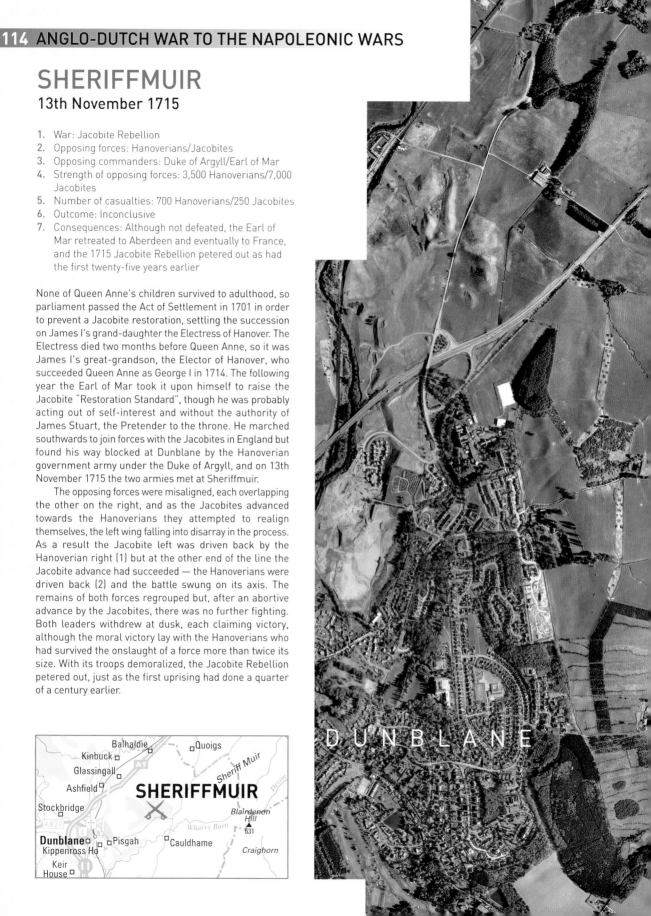

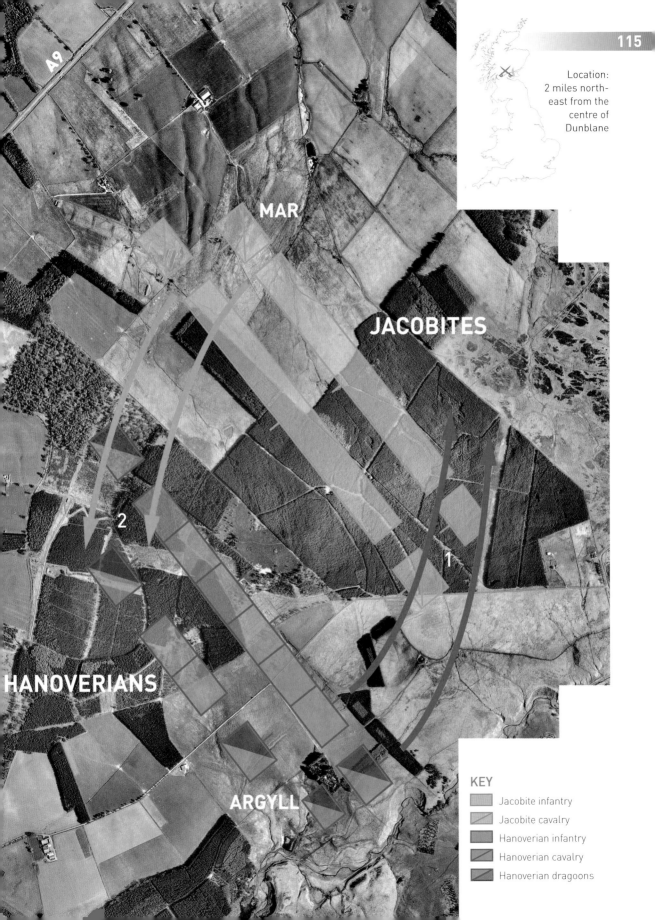

Location:
2 miles north-
east from the
centre of
Dunblane

A9

MAR

JACOBITES

2

1

HANOVERIANS

ARGYLL

KEY

Jacobite infantry

Jacobite cavalry

Hanoverian infantry

Hanoverian cavalry

Hanoverian dragoons

CULLODEN
16th April 1746

1. War: Jacobite Rebellion
2. Opposing forces: Hanoverians/Jacobites
3. Opposing commanders: Duke of Cumberland/Charles Stuart
4. Strength of opposing forces: 9,000 Hanoverians/5,000 Jacobites
5. Number of casualties: 360 Hanoverians/1000 Jacobites
6. Outcome: Hanoverian victory
7. Consequences: Charles Stuart fled to France and the Jacobite cause was at an end

It was to be thirty years after the failed rising of 1715 (see p. 114) before Jacobite took to the field once more. This time the uprising centred around Charles Stuart (Bonnie Prince Charlie), who landed in Scotland in August 1745. The British Army was beaten by the Jacobites at Prestonpans in September 1745 and at Falkirk in January 1746. The Jacobite army failed to capitalize on these successes and withdrew to Inverness, where they waited for the approaching Hanoverians, under the command of the Duke of Cumberland. On 15th April 1746, the Jacobites deployed for battle on Drummossie Muir, close to Culloden Park, but the Hanoverians declined to do battle that day. Charles Stuart, taking personal charge of the Jacobite forces, resolved on a night attack on the Hanoverian camp. But his forces lost their way in the darkness, and returned exhausted to their original positions at dawn on 16th April (1) to face the enemy who deployed opposite (2) with several detachments hidden behind a wall to the south (3).

The battle began with a cannonade that decimated the already inferior Jacobite numbers, a situation exacerbated by Bonnie Prince Charlie's hesitancy to order a charge. Eventually Lord George Murray launched a cavalry charge on his own initiative (4) and was followed by the Jacobite centre (5), the momentum of whose charge was lost to the boggy ground and who found themselves attacked from the flank by the concealed Hanoverian detachments. Hanoverian dragoons now attacked Prince Charles's cavalry and, finding himself in severe danger, the Prince withdrew from the field. With that, Jacobite resistance crumbled and the Highlanders found themselves slaughtered by an enemy who had been ordered to show no mercy. The last battle of the Jacobite Rebellions, and the last pitched battle to be fought on British soil, had lasted less than an hour.

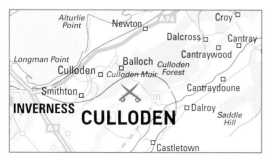

KEY

Jacobite infantry

Jacobite cavalry

Government infantry

Government cavalry

Government dragoons

◀ viewpoint

P car park

⊥ monument

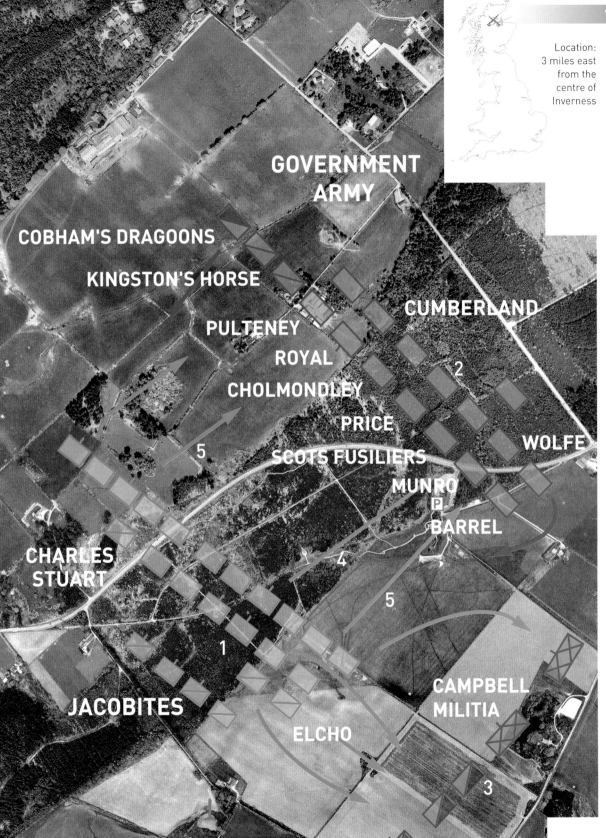

GOVERNMENT
ARMY

COBHAM'S DRAGOONS

KINGSTON'S HORSE

CUMBERLAND

PULTENEY

ROYAL

CHOLMONDLEY

2

PRICE

SCOTS FUSILIERS

WOLFE

5

MUNRO

BARREL

CHARLES
STUART

4

5

1

CAMPBELL
MILITIA

JACOBITES

ELCHO

3

MARTELLO TOWERS
1805-12

1. War: Napoleonic Wars
2. Opposing forces: Britain/France
3. Opposing commanders: Lord Nelson/Napoleon Bonaparte
4. Strength of opposing forces: 130,000-strong French invasion force
5. Number of casualties: None on British soil
6. Outcome: Invasion prevented by Nelson's blockade
7. Consequences: The Martello towers were built to counter the threat of an invasion that never came, and were never put to the test

England Photographic Atlas: Page 181, E4

Four years after the French Revolution, the new republic, seeking to expand its territories, declared war on England. Napoleon threatened to invade, and by 1804 he had amassed a 130,000-strong invasion force at Calais. The only thing that stood between Napoleon and his dream was Nelson's navy – the British government knew that it must strengthen its coastal defences in case the French Navy managed to dodge Nelson's blockade, and so began the building of Britain's biggest ever coastal defence system.

Inspired by a fortified tower at Cape Mortella on Corsica that had withstood bombardment from two British battleships in 1794, military engineer Captain William Ford proposed a chain of such towers stretching from Dover to Newhaven on the south coast, and a second chain stretching from Brightlingsea to Aldeburgh on the east. Work on the south coast towers began in spring 1805 and continued even after Nelson's destruction of the French fleet at the Battle of Trafalgar on October 21st because, although Napoleon withdrew his forces from Calais, he had vowed to return to fulfil his plan of invasion. 73 Martello towers had been erected along the south coast by 1808, with additional forts at Dymchurch and Eastbourne, while a further 29 Martello towers were built on the east coast between 1808 and 1812. (Tower 74 in the south coast chain was later erected at Seaford.)

Three years after the completion of this massive chain of towers, on 18th June 1815, Napoleon was defeated by Wellington at Waterloo and the threat of invasion was finally dispelled without any of the Martello towers having been put to the test. During the Second World War many of the towers were requisitioned as part of the coastal defences against the threat of invasion by Hitler.

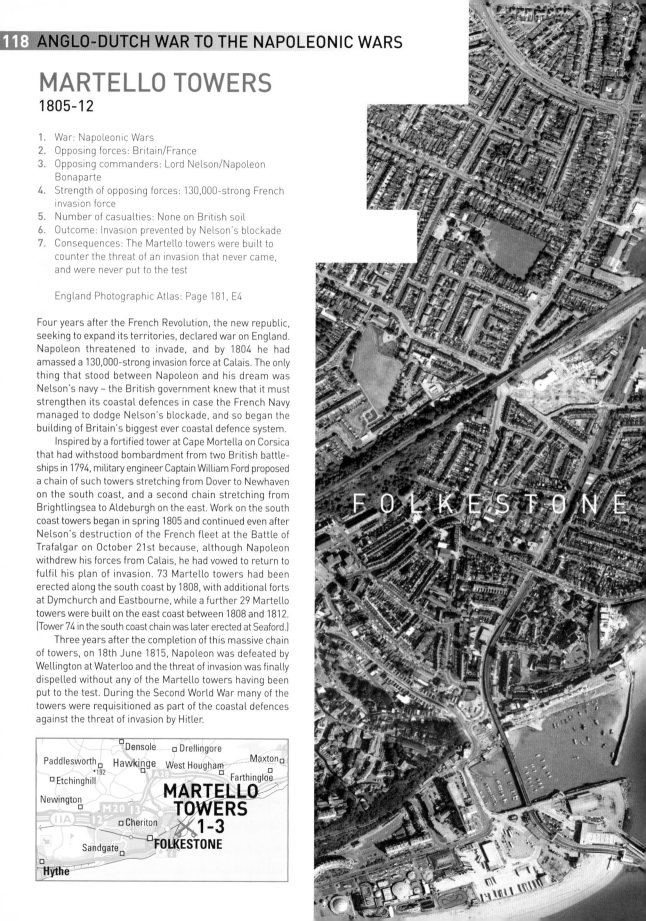

FOLKESTONE

Location:
0.5 miles west
from the
centre of
Folkestone

Tower 1

Tower 2

Tower 3

WWI/II AND DESERT STORM

LONDON AIR RAIDS
July 1915 – May 1918

1. War: First World War
2. Opposing forces: Luftwaffe/Royal Flying Corps/Royal Air Force
3. Strength of opposing forces: Raids by Zeppelins and, from June 1917, the Gotha IV long-range bomber
4. Number of casualties: 835 dead and 1,437 injured
5. Outcome: Air raids failed to bomb Britain into suing for peace
6. Consequences: Anti-aircraft defences were implemented and the Royal Flying Corps and Royal Naval Air Service were amalgamated to form the Royal Air Force

England Photographic Atlas: Pages 235–6

During the First World War Britain faced a new kind of threat – aerial warfare – and for the first time civilians experienced the horrors of war first hand. The intention of German air raids on London and the surrounding counties was to bludgeon the British public into forcing the government to sue for peace, and while the Luftwaffe did not achieve this aim it did succeed in undermining morale, reducing industrial production by up to 25% in the areas that were bombed, and causing a public outcry at the lack of aerial defence.

The first of fifty-two First World War air raids on Britain came on the night of 31st May 1915, when a Zeppelin airship dropped incendiary devices from Stoke Newington to Stepney, killing six and injuring thirty-five people. Although the public complained at the lack of aerial defence, one of the Royal Flying Corps' successes came on 3rd September 1916, when William Leefe Robinson shot down a Zeppelin during an air raid on London.

Zeppelin raids had a relatively limited effect, but from June 1917 raids by the Gotha IV long-range bomber were far more devastating. In all 835 people were killed and 1,437 injured, and Britain began to build up an air defence system. Major cities were protected by anti-aircraft guns and searchlights, and in 1918 the Royal Flying Corps and Royal Naval Air Service were amalgamated to form the Royal Air Force. The RAF provided fighter cover to prevent air raids on cities, and by the end of the war had become the largest air force in the world.

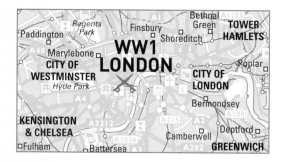

✴ Approximate position of bombs dropped during the Gotha raids, from June 1917

Location:
central
London

LONDON (THE BLITZ)
29th December 1940

1. War: Second World War
2. Opposing forces: Luftwaffe/Royal Air Force
3. Opposing commanders: Reichsmarschall Hermann Goering/Air Chief Marshal Sir Hugh Dowding
4. Strength of opposing forces: c. 300 Luftwaffe aircraft per raid
5. Number of casualties: 20,000 killed and 25,000 injured in 71 air raids on London between September 1940 and May 1941
6. Outcome: The Luftwaffe failed to bomb London into submission
7. Consequences: Although Hitler succeeded in destroying factories and buildings, disrupting services and production, the Blitz strengthened rather than weakened British resolve to continue the war

London Photographic Atlas: Page 2-3

The word "Blitz" is derived from the German word blitzkrieg, meaning "lightning war", but in fact the repeated night-time air raids that constituted the Blitz were anything but lightning war: they were part of a long, slow process of attrition intended to demoralize and disable London and, when that failed, other British cities. For London, the night of 7th September 1940, "Black Saturday", marked the start of 76 nights of consecutive bombing relieved only on 2nd November when bad weather grounded the Luftwaffe.

After that the targets changed to other cities, including Coventry, and between 18th November 1940 and 19th January 1941 London suffered only six full scale night raids – but that of December 29th was more destructive than any previous attack. It is said that only bad weather over the German airfields, which prevented the Luftwaffe from following up the initial attack, saved London from total destruction. Close concentrations of incendiary devices set ablaze the City of London, the City of Westminster and the Isle of Dogs, while high explosives fell from Hornsey in the north to Bromley in the south and from Kingston in the west to Woolwich and Chislehurst in the east, with the highest concentration over the City, Southwark and Bermondsey.

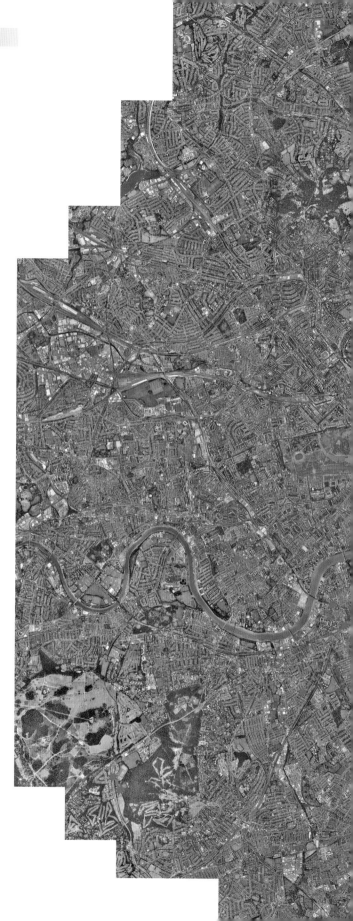

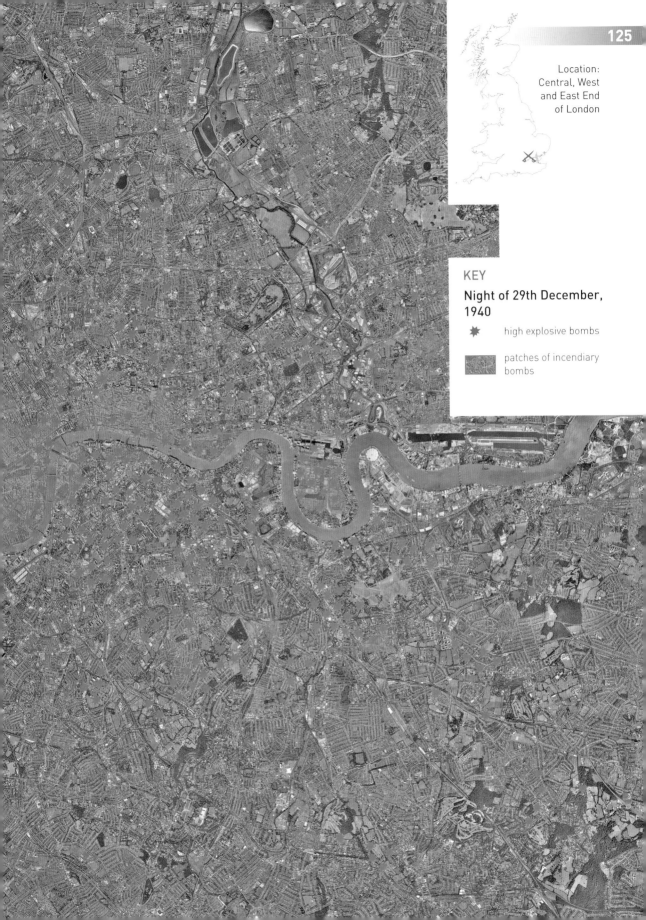

Location:
Central, West
and East End
of London

KEY

Night of 29th December, 1940

✴ high explosive bombs

patches of incendiary bombs

EXERCISE TIGER
22nd-30th April 1944

1. War: Second World War
2. Opposing forces: Britain and USA/Germany
3. Opposing commanders: Admiral Don P. Moon/Routine patrol
4. Strength of opposing forces: 8 US landing craft/9 German E-boats
5. Number of casualties: 749 US personnel
6. Outcome: German success
7. Consequences: News of this disastrous D-Day rehearsal was kept secret so as not to jeopardise the actual Normandy landings

England Photographic Atlas: Page 31, F&G 4-6

In December 1943 the US Army began training exercises at Slapton Sands for the forthcoming Normandy landings. This particular area was chosen because the terrain, with a coarse gravel beach, shallow lagoon and bluffs, closely resembled the Normandy beaches. The people living in the nearby villages were evacuated and the troops began a long, highly secretive training that culminated in two full-scale rehearsals of the Normandy landings, the first one code-named Tiger.

Exercise Tiger was the rehearsal for the Utah Beach assault under the command of Admiral Don P. Moon, held from 22nd to 30th April 1944. After marshalling and embarkation, the main force bombarded Slapton Sands in the early hours of 27th April and made its landings the same morning. The follow-up convoy of 8 landing craft left Brixham and Plymouth 24 hours later but, as the convoy approached Slapton Sands in the small hours of 28th April, it was attacked by 9 German E-boats that had evaded the Allied patrols. Two landing craft were torpedoed with the loss of 749 lives, making Tiger the most disastrous training exercise of the war. In order to keep Allied plans secret, details of the disaster were not released until after the invasion, and even doctors and nurses treating the injured were sworn to secrecy.

Ten years after the successful Normandy landings on D-Day, 6th June 1944, the US Army unveiled a monument at Slapton Sands thanking the local people who had "generously left their homes and their lands to provide a battle practice area for the successful assault in Normandy", and honouring those who had died in this tragic exercise.

Location: 6 miles east from the centre of Kingsbridge

monument

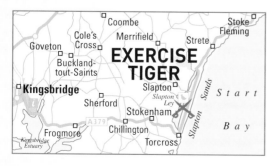

RAF LYNEHAM
August 1990-April 1991

1. War: Gulf War
2. Opposing forces: Iraq/World Coalition of 29 countries
3. Opposing commanders: Saddam Hussein/General Norman Schwarzkopf
4. Strength of opposing forces: up to 545,000 Iraqis/over 270,000 Coalition
5. Number of casualties: 400,000 Iraqis/148 Coalition
6. Outcome: Coalition victory
7. Consequences: Iraq was forced to withdraw from Kuwait and was subject to economic sanctions and weapons inspections

England Photographic Atlas: Page 105, E3

Location: 10 miles northwest from the centre of Chippenham

RAF Lyneham, home of the RAF's tactical transport fleet of Hercules aircraft, played a large role in all three phases of the Gulf War, during Operation Granby (the build-up to hostilities), Operation Desert Storm (the assault itself), and during the post-war supply of humanitarian aid to Kurdish refugees in Northern Iraq. During Operation Granby, which began on August 6th 1990 and lasted until the ground invasion of February 24th 1991, 40,000 hours and 12,000,000 miles were flown by the aircraft of Lyneham Transport Wing, carrying 50,000 tons of equipment and supplies.

On 2nd August 1990, Iraq invaded Kuwait, and six days later the Iraqi dictator Saddam Hussein claimed the tiny state as part of Iraq. President George Bush secured the support of 28 nations to join the US in a coalition against Iraq and on 29th November the United Nations Security Council announced a deadline of 15th January for the Iraqi forces to leave Kuwait. Two days after the deadline, on 17th January, the coalition began an aerial bombardment, followed up by a ground attack on 24th February. US intelligence had greatly over-estimated the strength of Saddam Hussein's forces which capitulated almost immediately with very little resistance. Kuwait was liberated within four days and a cease-fire, called on 28th February, was made permanent on 11th April.

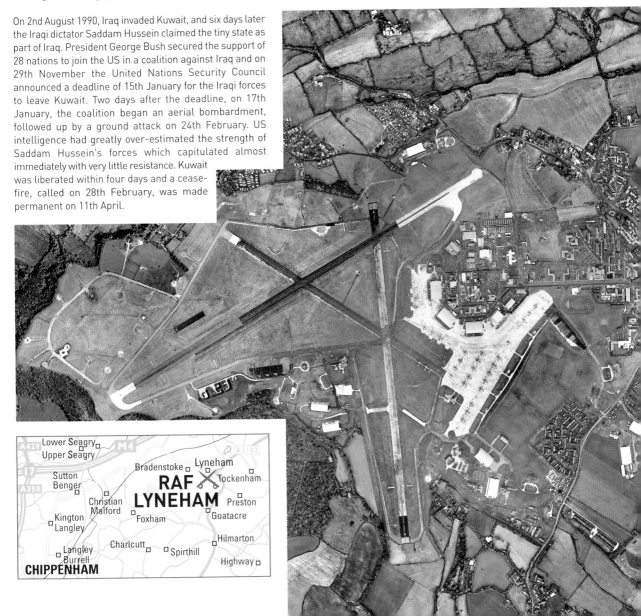

index